Breeding Bird Monitoring Protocol for the Heartland Network Inventory and Monitoring Program

Natural Resource Report NPS/HTLN/NRR—2008/044

David G. Peitz, Gareth A. Rowell, Jennifer L. Haack, Kevin M. James, Lloyd W. Morrison, and Mike D. DeBacker

National Park Service
Heartland I&M Network
Wilson's Creek National Battlefield
6424 West Farm Road 182
Republic, MO 65738

May 2008

U.S. Department of the Interior
National Park Service
Natural Resource Program Center
Fort Collins, Colorado

The Natural Resource Publication series addresses natural resource topics that are of interest and applicability to a broad readership in the National Park Service and to others in the management of natural resources, including the scientific community, the public, and the NPS conservation and environmental constituencies. Manuscripts are peer-reviewed to ensure that the information is scientifically credible, technically accurate, appropriately written for the intended audience, and is designed and published in a professional manner.

Natural Resource Reports are the designated medium for disseminating high priority, current natural resource management information with managerial application. The series targets a general, diverse audience, and may contain NPS policy considerations or address sensitive issues of management applicability. Examples of the diverse array of reports published in this series include vital signs monitoring plans; monitoring protocols; "how to" resource management papers; proceedings of resource management workshops or conferences; annual reports of resource programs or divisions of the Natural Resource Program Center; resource action plans; fact sheets; and regularly-published newsletters.

Views, statements, findings, conclusions, recommendations and data in this report are solely those of the author(s) and do not necessarily reflect views and policies of the U.S. Department of the Interior, National Park Service. Mention of trade names or commercial products does not constitute endorsement or recommendation for use by the National Park Service.

Printed copies of reports in these series may be produced in a limited quantity and they are only available as long as the supply lasts. This report is also available from the Heartland I&M Network and NRPM websites (http://www.nature.nps.gov/im/units/HTLN and http://www.nature.nps.gov/publications/NRPM/index.cfm, respectively) on the internet, or by sending a request to the address on the back cover.

Please cite this publication as:

Peitz, D.G., G.A. Rowell, J.L. Haack, K.M. James, L.W. Morrison, and M.D. DeBacker. 2008. Breeding Bird Monitoring Protocol for the Heartland Network Inventory and Monitoring Program. Natural Resource Report NPS/HTLN/NRR—2008/044. National Park Service, Fort Collins, Colorado.

NPS D-78, May 2008

Acknowledgements

The National Park Service's Inventory and Monitoring Program provided funding for bird monitoring protocol development and continues to fund monitoring across Heartland Network Inventory and Monitoring Program parks. The original edition of the protocol "Bird Monitoring Protocol for Agate Fossil Beds National Monument, Nebraska and Tallgrass Prairie National Preserve, Kansas" was written in 2003 by David G. Peitz, Steve G. Fancy, Lisa P. Thomas, Gareth A. Rowell and Mike D. DeBacker. Peer review of the original protocol was conducted by Drs. John Sauer (USGS Patuxent Wildlife Research Center), Rich Camps (USGS Pacific Island Ecosystems Research Center) and Rodney Sigel (Institute for Bird Populations). We have updated the protocol to reflect the network's expansion of its bird monitoring efforts into additional parks and the turning over of Agate Fossil Beds National Monument to the Northern Great Plains Inventory and Monitoring Network. This protocol uses sections of text without citation from the original protocol. Numerous NPS staff and volunteers have contributed to the development of this protocol. Therefore, the list of authors simply reflects those who put down on paper the work of this larger group.

Content

List of Figures

List of Tables

Breeding Bird Monitoring Protocol for the Heartland Network Inventory and Monitoring Program

1. Background and Objectives

1a. Issue Being Addressed and Rationale for Monitoring Bird Populations

Birds are an important component of park ecosystems, and their high body temperature, rapid metabolism, and high ecological position in most food webs make them a good indicator of the effects of local and regional changes in ecosystems. It has been suggested that management activities aimed at preserving habitat for bird populations, such as for neotropical migrants, can have the added benefit of preserving entire ecosystems and their attendant ecosystem services (Karr 1991, Maurer 1993). Moreover, birds have a tremendous following among the public, and many parks provide information on the status and trends of birds through their interpretive programs.

Native Great Plains grasslands and their constituent avian fauna once covered vast areas of the North American continent, in which the Heartland Network Inventory and Monitoring Program (HTLN) resides. During the last century, large portions of grassland landscapes were plowed for cropland or converted to livestock pasture (29% of shortgrass, 41% of mixed-grass, and 99% of tallgrass prairie; Knopf and Sampson 1997). Remaining grasslands have been altered further through continued fragmentation and isolation, changing agricultural practices, forest encroachment, interruption of driving ecological processes such as periodic wildfire, and loss of significant faunal species, including bison (*Bos bison*), elk (*Cervus elaphus*), and wolves (*Canis lupus*).

Parts of five physiographic areas identified by Partners In Flight (a bird conservation effort among federal, state and local government agencies, professional and private groups, industry and the academic community) are found within the grasslands of the HTLN (Figure 1). Each physiographic area has its unique habitat and suite of birds in need of conservation. The eastern-most of these physiographic areas is the Prairie Peninsula (31) with its gently rolling glacial plain in the west and flatter areas in the east. Historically, tallgrass prairie, savannah, and forest habitats were interspersed throughout the Prairie Peninsula. Central to the grasslands of the HTLN is the Dissected Till Plains physiographic area (32). This area was glaciated, uplifted, and subsequently eroded into a flat-to-rolling terrain that slopes gently toward the Missouri and Mississippi River Valleys. Historically, vegetation is a mosaic of tallgrass prairie and oak-hickory forest with oak savannahs characteristic of transition zones. Bottomland hardwoods dominated the river valleys. The Dissected Till Plains is the most heavily altered grassland area. The Osage Plains physiographic area (33) is the western and southern most of the three major grassland physiographic areas. It grades into savannah and woodland to the east and south, and into shorter mixed-grass prairie to the west. Two other grassland areas are found in parts of the northern extent of the HTLN; the Upper Great Lakes Plain (16) with its glacial moraines and dissected plateaus, and the Northern Tallgrass (40) with its prairie potholes. A variety of prairie communities, oak savannahs and broadleaf forest historically covered the Upper Great Lakes

Plain. Tallgrass prairie of varying heights was found throughout the Northern Tallgrass physiographic area.

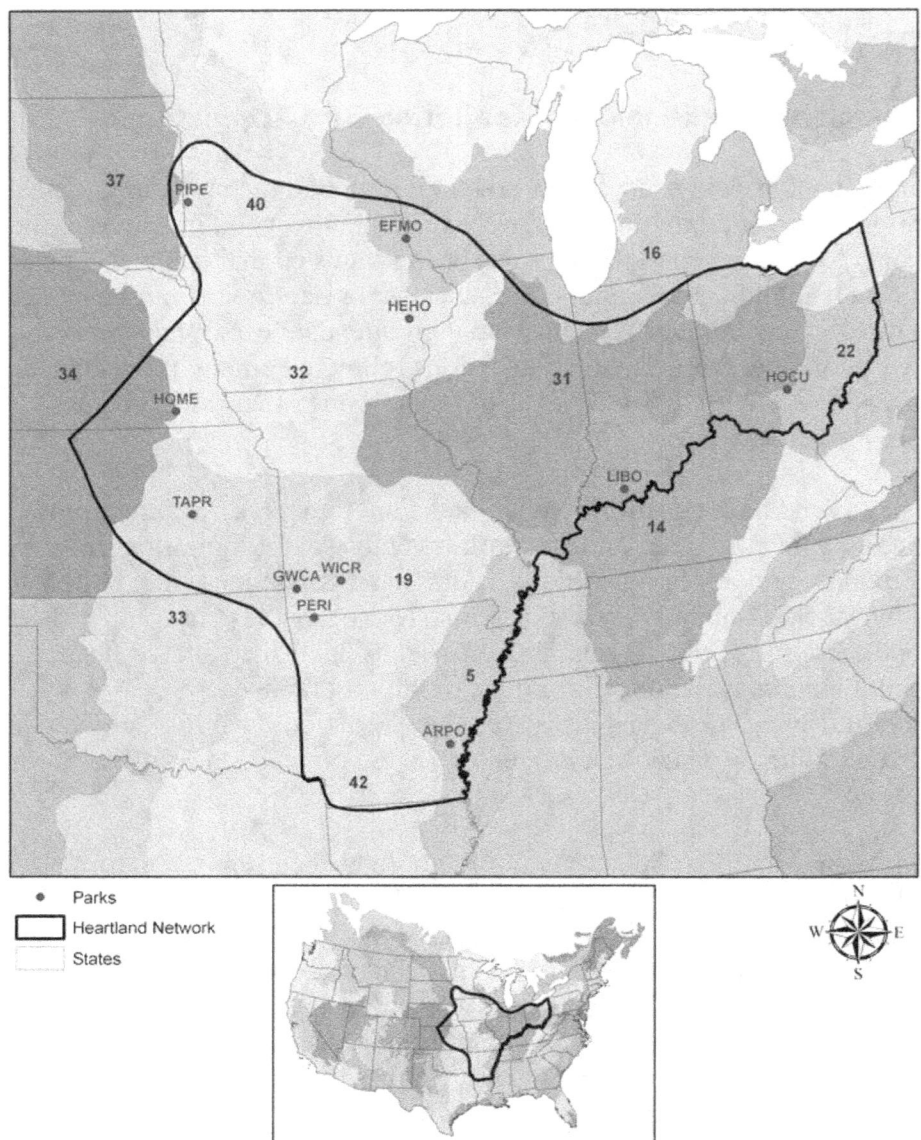

Figure 1. Physiographic areas identified by Partners In Flight found within the Heartland Network Inventory and Monitoring Program.

The far eastern section of the HTLN is within the Ohio Hills physiographic area (22), which consists primarily of unglaciated plateaus, valleys and mountains. The Ohio Hills were dominated historically by oak-hickory forests. The south-central section of the HTLN, the Ozark/Ouachita physiographic area (19), is mountainous as well. The Ozarks consist of three dissected plateaus covered with oak-dominated forests with glade and savannah inclusions. The Ouachitas are a ridge and valley system historically covered with shortleaf pine and interspersed with deciduous forest. The Ozark/Ouachita physiographic area is similar in many respects to the

Interior Low Plateaus (14) found in the southeastern section of the HTLN. Topography of the Interior Low Plateaus is hilly and rolling, but includes swampy alluvial valleys, established rivers and streams and karst plains. This area contains a rich and diverse plant community, with species from both the Midwestern and eastern United States. Over 150 bird species nest in the Interior Low Plateaus, reflecting this areas diversity of habitats (Ford et al. 2000).

At the time of European settlement, bottomland hardwood forest covered the last physiographic area found in the HTLN, the Mississippi Alluvial Valley (05; Twedt et al. 1999). Though dominated by bottomland hardwoods, isolated pockets of prairie could be found at higher elevations. Eighty percent of this forested land and most, if not all, the prairie land had been cleared for agricultural purposes. This drastically altered the hydrology of the land, further inhibiting many aspects of the ecosystem's integrity. The remaining forest was in small fragments, further reducing the capacity of the landscape to support bird populations. However, in recent years, forest clearing has essentially stopped and restoration of bottomland hardwood forest is increasing total forest coverage (Smith et al. 2004).

While not to the extent of large native ungulates and mammalian predators, many avian species have demonstrated declining abundance as habitat loss continues. Data collected during the U.S. Geological Survey's annual North American Breeding Bird Surveys (BBS) between 1966 and 1999 indicate that 70% of 29 grassland bird species show evidence of population declines (Sauer et al. 2000). Many prairie species such as the grasshopper sparrow (*Ammodramus savannarum*), eastern meadowlark (*Sturnella magna*), horned lark (*Eremophila alpestris*), bobolink (*Dolichonyx oryzivorus*), lark bunting (*Calamospiza melanocrys*), and dickcissel (*Spiza americana*) have declined at alarming rates (Sauer et al. 2003). The destruction and fragmentation of prairie landscapes, as well as the structural degradation resulting from fire suppression and changes in grazing regimes of remaining prairie habitats, contribute to these declines. Woodland bird species, especially neotropical warblers, have undergone even more precipitous declines related to habitat loss. Partners in Flight lists 29 different species that breed in one or more physiographic areas of the HTLN in need of conservation. Species are listed in need of conservation because of low population numbers and/or threats to the unique habitat they require. National Park Service lands are well suited for avian species conservation as they are often managed to preserve unique habitats that are under-represented at the landscape scale but are vital to a species survival.

It is against a backdrop of vanishing or altered ecosystems, declining bird populations and the unique role that National Park Service lands can play in conserving threatened bird species that we propose monitoring avian communities on National Park Service lands within the HTLN. Long-term trends in the community composition and abundance of breeding bird populations provide one measure for assessing the ecological integrity and sustainability of ecosystems. Long-term patterns in community composition and species abundance in relation to changes in the structural diversity of vegetation will improve our understanding of the effects of various management actions.

1b. Historical Development of Bird Monitoring in Network Parks

In prairies, trends in the composition and abundance of grassland bird populations have been proposed as a long-term indicator of ecosystem integrity, which is defined as the capability to support and maintain a balanced, integrated, adaptive community of organisms having a community composition, diversity, and functional organization comparable to that of natural habitat of the region (Karr and Dudley 1981). During 1998 and 1999, as part of the design phase of the Prairie Cluster Prototype Long-term Ecological Monitoring Program (PC-LTEM) led by the U.S. Geological Survey (USGS), bird inventories and pilot monitoring work was conducted in eight prairie parks by Dr. Powell of the USGS, to identify the species present at each park and assess the feasibility of using grassland birds as indicators of ecosystem integrity (Powell 2000). Work was conducted at Agate Fossil Beds National Monument, Nebraska (AGFO); Badlands National Park, South Dakota (BADL), Homestead National Monument of America, Nebraska (HOME); Pipestone National Monument, Minnesota (PIPE); Scotts Bluff National Monument, Nebraska (SCBL); Tallgrass Prairie National Preserve, Kansas (TAPR); Theodore Roosevelt National Park, North Dakota (THRO) and Wilson's Creek National Battlefield, Missouri (WICR).

As a follow-up to work done by Dr. Powell, the PC-LTEM Program initiated a pilot bird monitoring project in the spring of 2001 to monitor avian communities at AGFO and TAPR. A culmination of this pilot project was a bird monitoring protocol completed in July 2003 (see Peitz et al. 2003), and a bird monitoring program for the PC-LTEM Program. With the merger of the PC-LTEM Program and the HTLN, bird monitoring was expanded to Herbert Hoover National Historic Site, Iowa (HEHO) and Hopewell Culture National Historical Site, Ohio (HOCU) in 2005. Arkansas Post National Memorial, Arkansas (ARPO) and Lincoln Boyhood National Memorial, Indiana (LIBO) were added in 2007. George Washington Carver National Monument, Missouri (GWCA); Pea Ridge National Military Park, Arkansas (PERI); and WICR will be added to HTLN bird monitoring efforts in 2008 and Effigy Mounds National Monument, Iowa (EFMO); HOME; and PIPE in 2009. With the transfer of AGFO to the Northern Great Plains Network (NGPN), bird monitoring by the HTLN at AGFO ceased in 2006.

Initially, habitat data was collected on four subplots per variable circular plot (VCP) plot surveyed. To facilitate the expansion of bird monitoring across network parks, we reduced the number of subplots sampled from four to one. Analysis of existing data showed that multiple subplots did not provide enough additional information to justify continued sampling. Analysis also demonstrated that habitat was very uniform within habitat types, and, as such, was a poor predictor of species occurrence. Changes over time of bird habitat will be correlated with trends in species density at the park scale (see Appendix D).

1c. Measurable Objectives

There are two primary objectives for the monitoring described in this protocol:

1. Identify significant temporal changes in composition and abundance of bird communities in 11 parks within the HTLN during the breeding season.

2. Improve our understanding of breeding bird – habitat relationships and the effects of management actions such as grazing, exotic plant removal and prescribed fire regimes on bird populations, by correlating changes in bird community composition and abundance with changes in habitat variables.

2. Sampling Design

2a. Rationale for Selecting This Sampling Design over Others

Hundreds of different sampling approaches have been used to quantify status or trends in bird populations and dozens of different monitoring programs are currently in place throughout North America to determine local, regional, or national trends in bird numbers. Most common survey methods allow simultaneous collection of information about species that share a common life history or habitat, but no single method will adequately sample the diversity of either habitats that birds occupy or life history groups such as seabirds, songbirds, raptors and shorebirds.

The sampling design described in this protocol involves a series of sampling stations laid out on a systematic grid that are sampled during 5-minute counts using the variable circular plot (VCP) methodology (Reynolds et al. 1980, Scott et al. 1986, Buckland et al. 1993, 2001, Fancy 1997, Nelson and Fancy 1999). Variable circular plots and line transect sampling are two types of distance sampling. Distance sampling has been used for more than 30 years to estimate animal abundance and is the best omnibus method currently available for determining relative abundance or trends for birds in most sampling situations. In practice, the method documented in this protocol is basically the same as point counts, such as those used in the Breeding Bird Survey (BBS), except that for each bird heard or seen during the count, its horizontal distance from the observer is estimated. In the case of line transect sampling, the observer walks down a transect and records either the perpendicular distance to each bird heard or seen, or else records the sighting angle and sighting distance instead of the perpendicular distance. Line transects are usually more efficient than VCP counts where they can be conducted because the observer collects data continuously while walking along the transect, whereas during VCP counts the observer only records birds detected during 3-10 minute sampling periods from stations located along a transect or on a systematic grid. However, VCP counts are the preferred approach in patchy habitats where correlations between bird data and vegetation or other habitat information are sought and in dense, rugged or hazardous terrain where you need to watch your footing as you traverse the landscape. Another advantage of VCP counts is that data can be directly compared to historical point count data such as those obtained during BBS counts and can contribute to ongoing programs such as the National Point Count Database. A summary of the advantages and disadvantages of the VCP method in relation to other techniques can be found in Bibby et al. (2000).

An important benefit of using the variable circular plot method is the ability to accommodate a wide range of bird species, each of which possesses a different singing style and each of which may occur in a variety of acoustically-different habitats (British Columbia Resource Inventory Branch {BCRIB} 1999). VCP counts operate by essentially allowing the habitat to determine the size of the area being surveyed. The maximum detectable distance to a bird may change between different habitats, but the radius of the survey will also change. For example, surveys of grassland birds usually cover a larger area per point because of the absence of a screen of trees, and because bird species may be flushed at greater distances in open habitats (BCRIB 1999).

In addition to the rationale for VCP counts given above, this protocol uses variable circular plot counts arranged in a systematic grid to address the two objectives for bird monitoring parks for the following reasons:

- A primary objective is to associate changes in bird community composition and abundance with long-term changes in vegetation that occur as a result of natural succession or various management actions (e.g., prescribed fire, grazing). We cannot (prior to the first year of the long-term sampling scheme) stratify the park into areas that will be subjected to different management regimes (e.g., grazed versus ungrazed) because the location and timing of future management will be based on feedback from adaptive management and other factors and cannot be predicted. Thus, the approach is to sample birds on a systematic grid that will allow inferences to be made to the entire park, and to later post-stratify the data to investigate changes in bird community composition and numbers as a result of different management regimes.

- Unadjusted point counts, such as those used in the Breeding Bird Survey, do not account for the number of birds missed during the counting interval. The number of birds that are counted at a sampling station is a combination of the number of birds that are actually there, and the proportion of them detected. Use of unadjusted point counts to calculate trends in abundance assumes that the proportion of birds detected is the same among species, observers and counting conditions, which is usually not the case. Without a measure of detectability, counts of birds are an unreliable measure of differences in the actual number of birds present (see Burnham 1981, Barker and Sauer 1995, Nelson and Fancy 1999). To obtain credible long-term trend data, and to allow comparisons among bird species and habitat types where detectability is expected to differ, we will incorporate distance measures to improve the quality of the data.

- By recording distances and by keeping track of whether a bird was detected during the first 3 minutes of the count or between minutes 3-5, we will be able to make direct comparisons between our data and those collected by others using the BBS or Ralph et al. (1995) methods.

- Our approach allows data from repeated surveys of the same area or areas with similar habitat characteristics to be combined to increase sample sizes. By combining surveys, it is possible to develop detection functions for uncommon species for which few detections are recorded during any single survey.

Occasionally, there are detectability issues in bird sampling that VCP and other estimation procedures cannot address. For example, there may be unobservable portions of the population (such as cryptic and silent females or nocturnal birds) that are not detected at all during counting, or it may be impossible to estimate detectability at the appropriate scale (e.g., when habitat-specific detectability exists in a rare species). In structurally complex habitats (e.g., forests in the northwest U.S. with very tall trees and multiple shrub and tree layers that make it impossible to see birds high up in the canopy directly above the observer) it may be difficult or impossible to detect birds at close horizontal distances to the observer. Thus, even with a measure of detectability factored into estimates derived from counts of birds, such estimates may still be an unreliable measure of differences in the actual number of birds present in some situations. However, it is important to note that although data may be less reliable for species encountered at low rates, it is still valuable to collect the data, and pooling of data over time may allow certain limited analyses. Interpretation of survey data requires sensitivity to these extra-statistical limitations of the estimation procedures.

2b. Site Selection

Sampling locations or 'plots' are selected as described in SOP #9.4, "Establishing and Marking Sampling Plots." Briefly, permanent sampling locations were selected by overlaying systematic grids (originating from a random starting point) on park maps (see Table 4.1). Systematic sampling across the park will allow us to make park-wide inferences concerning the avian community. The orientation of the systematic grid was rotated 45 degrees from north at: ARPO, GWCA, HOME, LIBO, PERI, PIPE and WICR to prevent sampling sites from being influenced by man-made features (roads, fences, etc.) oriented along cardinal directions. The systematic grid at EFMO and HEHO were rotated from north 8 and 52 degrees, respectively, to match existing vegetation grids. The angle of the sampling grid at TAPR was selected randomly and equals 34 degrees from north. The unique shapes of the different units at HOCU dictated that the systematic grid be oriented in cardinal directions. At TAPR the riparian corridor was identified as a separate stratum, with sampling extending 125 m on either side of the stream channel (Palmer and Fox Creeks). The riparian stratum makes up 5.3% of the total park area (4398 ha) at TAPR. Within the riparian stratum, plots were located at 250 m intervals along the extent of the stream. Any plots from the overall park grid that fell within the riparian stratum were discarded. A total of 771 plots were established in parks across the HTLN (Table 1). Sampling locations are not physically marked on the ground; rather UTM coordinates are maintained and located in the field with a GPS unit. Refer to SOP #9.3 "Using GPS" and SOP #9.4 "Establishing and Marking Sampling Plots" for navigation between sampling plots and plot establishment instructions.

This systematic approach to selecting sampling sites allows flexibility to choose the appropriate reference frame to answer different monitoring questions. When making park-wide inferences, results from each stratum at TAPR will be weighted by area and combined to give an overall park mean and variance. At the same time, more intensive sampling in the riparian corridor will ensure an adequate sample to describe habitat relationships specific to this less common, but important stratum. The systematic grid will also allow us to limit the reference frame appropriately when asking more specific monitoring questions (e.g. only those sampling points within particular management units would be used to compare the avian response to different fire or grazing regimes, etc.).

2c. Population Being Monitored

Sampling will be limited to the bird-breeding season (early May through mid-June), and sampling will include those species that may potentially breed in the park (see Appendix C).

Thus, the population being sampled includes breeding bird species within the park boundary that are present during the survey period.

2d. Sampling Frequency and Replication

For all parks included in the bird monitoring program, HTLN staff will survey birds on a four year rotating cycle, with some parks having additional sampling in the first two years (Table 1). Each individual bird plot will be visited once during a survey year.

Table 1. Sampling schedule for breeding bird surveys in the Heartland Network Inventory and Monitoring Program parks, 2008 through 2017. After 2009, all parks will be visited on a [1-3] sampling schedule.

Park / Plots	2008	2009	2010	2011	2012	2013	2014	2015	2016	2017
ARPO / 36	--	--	--	36	--	--	--	36	--	--
EFMO / 52	--	52	--	--	--	52	--	--	--	52
GWCA / 70	70	--	--	--	70	--	--	--	70	--
HEHO / 38	--	38	--	--	--	38	--	--	--	38
HOCU / 27	--	--	--	27	--	--	--	27	--	--
HOME / 48	--	48	--	--	--	48	--	--	--	48
LIBO / 35	--	--	--	35	--	--	--	35	--	--
PERI / 99	99	--	--	--	99	--	--	--	99	--
PIPE / 68	--	68	--	--	--	68	--	--	--	68
TAPR / 260	98	40	260	--	--	--	260	--	--	--
WICR / 38	38	--	--	--	38	--	--	--	38	--
TOTAL	**305 / 4**	**246 / 5**	**260 / 1**	**98 / 3**	**207 / 3**	**206 / 4**	**260 / 1**	**98 / 3**	**207 / 3**	**206 / 4**

3. Field Methods

3a. Field Season Preparations, Field Schedule and Equipment Setup

Prior to the field season each year, usually beginning in March or April, the observer(s) should review this entire protocol, including all of the SOPs. The observer should pay special attention to the tasks described in SOP #9.1 "Before the Field Season" and SOP #9.2 "Training Observers." Review of bird identification by sight and sound (see SOP #9.2) is particularly important each year, as the misidentification of a species is perhaps the most serious error one can make during a bird count, with greater consequences than errors in estimating distances or double-counting a bird. All of the equipment and supplies listed in SOP #9.1 should be organized and made ready for the field season, and copies of the field data forms in SOP #9.5 "Conducting the Variable Circular Plot Count" and SOP #9.6 "Documenting Habitat Variables" should be made, 25% of which should be on write-in-the-rain paper.

Staff workloads and unpredictable weather (e.g. delays in the onset of spring, periods of rain, spring storms) necessitate maintaining some flexibility in scheduling the sequence and duration of sampling trips. Sampling dates should be scheduled and logistics organized prior to the start of each field season. Twelve to fifteen VCP counts should be scheduled for completion each field day. Field trips up to 12 days in length will be necessary to complete bird surveys within the breeding season. To accommodate differences in vegetation phenology, parks should be visited in a south to north progression.

3b. Sampling Methods

The protocol generates two data sets collected concurrently; bird abundance (VCP) and habitat measures. The bird crew should arrive at the park the afternoon prior to the first day of sampling to familiarize themselves with the area and the birds present. Each night, the group discusses the next day's plans and establishes the route for visiting bird plots. The birding crew arrives at the first plot each day before sunrise and begins sampling as soon as it is light enough to do so. The habitat crew follows the route of the bird observer, being careful to avoid walking to the next plot until bird observations are completed and the observer has moved on. Habitat sampling on a plot commences after bird observations are complete. Loud voices, motion, or walking through a plot may disrupt the birds and bias survey results. The bird observer completes counts approximately four hours after local sunrise and then joins the habitat crew. Each day, the habitat crew attempts to complete habitat work on all plots sampled for birds that morning. However, this is not always possible and some plots may need to be sampled at a later date. No habitat sampling should be scheduled after June 30. Refer to SOP #9.5 "Conducting the Variable Circular Plot Count" for conducting bird counts and SOP #9.6 "Documenting Habitat Variables" for measuring habitat work.

Before leaving the field each day, data sheets are checked for completeness and readability. All information pertinent to the plots sampled that day is recorded to avoid repeating or skipping sampling plots. The project manager is responsible for the safekeeping and organization of the data sheets, and ensuring that data are entered into the database.

3c. Conducting the Variable Circular Plot Count

Variable circular plot counts are a point count methodology that incorporate a measure of detectability into population estimates (Buckland et al. 2001). Details of how to conduct VCP counts during the breeding season and for filling in data forms are given in SOP #9.5 "Conducting the Variable Circular Plot Count" and are summarized here. All birds seen or heard at each plot are recorded during a 5 minute sampling period. Bird observations are separated into two time segments: those detected during the first 3 minutes of the count (to allow comparisons with BBS data), and any new birds detected during the final 2 minutes of the count. All birds, regardless of distance detected from the observer, are counted and recorded. For most species, each individual bird will be recorded as a separate observation. For species that usually occur in clusters or flocks, the appropriate unit to record is the cluster or flock size, and not the individual bird.

When we conduct a VCP count, we are attempting to get an "instantaneous count" of birds present. Birds flushed from the plot when approached by the observer should be recorded and the count started as soon as the observer is at plot center. The method takes into account the fact that birds close to the observer have a higher probability of being detected (if they are not flushed) than birds far from the observer, and that different species have different detection functions (i.e., the probability of detecting a bird at different distances from the observer). An important assumption of the method is that a bird exactly at the center of the plot has a 100% probability of being detected, and that there is a high probability of detecting birds within the first 5-10 m of the plot center. The most important birds to detect are those very close to the observer (within the first 5-10 m), and it is highly desirable that estimated distances be within 1-2 m of actual distances for any bird within 20 m of the observer. However, all birds seen or heard should be recorded with an estimate of distance from the observer. Distances should be estimated to the nearest meter in the field (during subsequent data analysis, distances will be grouped into intervals to lessen the effect of errors in estimating distances); distances should not be rounded to the nearest 5 or 10 m. Birds far from the center of the plot usually have little effect on the resulting distance function; during data analysis, 5-10% of the farthest detection distances for each species will be truncated before a detection function is calculated.

Once a count is completed at a plot and the data sheet filled out, the observer uses a GPS unit to navigate to the next plot. Twelve to fifteen plots can be sampled each morning during a period between when it is light enough to observe birds to four hours post sunrise.

3d. Collecting Habitat Data

Habitat data are collected in a 50-m radius plot centered on each sampling point and in one 5-m radius and 1.78-m radius nested subplots. SOP #9.6 "Documenting Habitat Variables" gives a detailed description of how habitat data are collected; a brief summary is presented here.

Habitat data are collected to meet several objectives. Large-scale plot attributes such as vegetation type, slope, and water cover are relevant to bird community composition and also place the plot in a landscape context. Canopy structure and horizontal vegetation profile data (collected at 5-m radius scale) characterize habitat structure available to birds and also link bird data to park vegetation types. Similarly, ground cover and foliar cover of vegetation guilds (collected at the 1.78-m radius scale) allow us to integrate bird monitoring with more in-depth vegetation data collected as part of plant community monitoring. Integrating these monitoring projects will allow us to provide feedback on how management actions influence vegetation, which in turn may affect bird community composition and abundance.

The collection of habitat data starts each morning after the first VCP count has been completed. The habitat crew samples VCP plots in the same order as the bird observer to avoid disturbing birds on plots where the bird count has not been conducted. The bird observer flags the center point of each VCP, making it easier for the habitat crew to find. The habitat crew navigates to the plots using one or more of the following: a GPS unit, compass and field map that includes compass bearings for the grid, or directions from the bird observer. Once the habitat crew arrives at a plot, they set up the subplots at plot center and complete all habitat measures for the subplots and for the 50-m radius plot.

4. Data Management

4a. Overview of Database Design

Effective data management allows the project leader to store and retrieve large quantities of data securely and efficiently. Data management especially becomes an issue when observational sample sizes are in the range of 10^4 to 10^5 or greater. Database design is critical to understanding how to use a database effectively. All data management activities related to this protocol are described in more detail in SOP #9.7 "Data Management."

The I&M Program designed the Natural Resource Database Template (NRDT) as a proof-of-concept database model for managing long-term ecological monitoring data. Two widely-distributed versions have been implemented in Access (National Park Service 2006). The database template has a core structure that standardizes the relationship between location and temporal data. The template promotes integration of I&M datasets and reduces database development time.

Microsoft Access 2003 is the primary software environment for managing the bird monitoring database. ArcGIS 9.2 (Environmental Systems Research Institute, Inc.) is used for managing spatial data associated with field sampling locations. Data and metadata products will be posted at the NPS I&M website, http://science.nature.nps.gov/nrgis. QA/QC guidelines in this document are based on recommendations of Rowell et al. (2005) and S. Fancy at http://science.nature.nps.gov/im/monitor/index.cfm and citations therein.

The database for bird monitoring has a hierarchical design based on NRDT. Locations and sampling periods are maintained at the top level of the database. Sampling periods represent monitoring seasons with a start and end date. The database includes (1) *bird observations and associated weather condition tables* -- which form the core data from the bird monitoring activities, and (2) *habitat sampling tables* -- which represent the seasonal vegetative conditions associated with the observed bird species. Each habitat data table can be joined with bird observations and exported for correlation and other analyses.

4b. Data Entry

A number of features have been designed into the database to minimize errors that occur when field data are transcribed to the database for storage and analysis. Forms are used as portals for data entry into the database. Standardized identifiers (*e.g.*, sample location and periods) are selected from a list of easily interpreted codes. Species and habitat data are entered into fields linked to appropriate tables. Look-up tables contain project-specific data and prohibit entry of data into a field if a corresponding value is not included in the look-up table. Consequently, only valid names or measures may be entered and spelling mistakes are eliminated. Species or habitat measures are selected using a pick list or by typing the beginning of the name.

4c. Data Verification and Editing

Data verification immediately follows data entry and involves checking the accuracy of computerized records against the original source, usually paper field records. While the goal of data entry is to achieve 100% correct entries, this is rarely accomplished. To minimize transcription errors, our policy is to verify 100% of records to their original source by staff familiar with project design and field implementation. Further, 10% of records are reviewed a second time by the project leader. If errors in excess of 3% are found in the project leader's review, then the entire data set is verified again. Once the computerized data are verified as accurately reflecting the original field data, the paper forms are archived and the electronic version is used for all subsequent data activities.

Although data may be correctly transcribed from the original field forms, they may not be accurate or logical. For example, a bird count of 233 instead of 23 may be illogical and almost certainly incorrect, whether or not it was properly transcribed from field forms. The process of reviewing computerized data for range and logic errors is the validation stage. Certain components of data validation are built into data entry forms (*e.g.*, range limits). Data validation can also be extended into the design and structure of the database. As much as possible, values for data-entry forms have been limited to valid entries stored in the look-up tables.

Additional data validation can be accomplished during verification, if the operator is sufficiently knowledgeable about the data. The project leader will validate the data after verification is complete. Validation procedures seek to identify generic errors (*e.g.*, missing, mismatched, or duplicate records) as well as errors specific to particular projects.

During the entry, verification, and validation phases, the project leader is responsible for the data. The project leader must assure consistency between field forms and the database by noting how and why any changes were made to the data on the original field forms. In general, changes made to the field forms should not be made via erasure, but rather through marginal notes or attached explanations. Once validation is complete, the data set is turned over to the data manager for archiving and storage.

Spatial validation of database sample coordinates can be accomplished using ArcGIS (ESRI, Inc.). Because this is an Access-maintained database, it can be converted into a geodatabase with ArcCatalog (ArcGIS, ESRI, Inc). Coordinate data (UTM northing and easting) of the locations table can then be used to validate the UTM coordinate values for sample locations stored in Access against the original GPS coordinates.

4d. Metadata Procedures

Metadata for project data are developed using the NPS Database Metadata Extractor (an Access add-in). This software utility provides output which follows current Federal Geographic Data Committee (FGDC) standards.

4e. Database Versions

Changes in database structure and functionality require a versioning system. This allows for the tracking of changes over time. With proper controls and communication, versioning ensures that only the most current version is used in any analysis. Versioning of archived data sets is handled by adding a two digit number separated by a period to the file name, with the first version being numbered 1.0. Minor changes such as revisions in forms and report content should be noted by an increase of the number to the right of the period. Major changes such as migration between Access versions or database normalization across multiple tables should be indicated by an increase in the number to the left of the period. Frequent users of the data are notified of the updates, and provided with a copy of the most recent archived version.

4f. Database Security

Secure data archiving is essential for protecting data files from corruption. No versions of the database should be deleted under any circumstance. Multiple backup copies of all program data are maintained at the HTLN offices, at the Wilson's Creek visitor center, and at the Missouri State University campus offices. Tape backups of the databases are made weekly. Each weekly full backup copy is maintained at the Wilson's Creek National Battlefield Visitor Center, Republic, Missouri. Once a month, one tape copy is stored offsite.

4g. Data Distribution

Currently, data are available for research and management applications on request, for database versions where all QA/QC has been completed and the data have been archived. Most data requests are currently met using FTP services. Portions of the monitoring data collected under this protocol will be made available for download directly from the NPS I&M Monitoring webpage. Information related to location and persistence of species determined to be threatened or endangered will not be made available for download by the general public. Data requests should be directed to:

Data Manager
Heartland I&M Network
National Park Service
Wilson's Creek National Battlefield
6424 W. Farm Rd. 182
Republic MO 65738-9514
(417) 732-6438

5. Analysis and Reporting

A critical component of any long-term monitoring protocol is a consistent and systematic way of analyzing and reporting on information (data) collected. This protocol has the stated goals of: 1) identifying significant temporal changes in composition and abundance of breeding bird communities and 2) determining breeding bird – habitat relationships and the effects of management actions. Therefore, analyses must be able to identify changes in breeding bird communities through time and relate these changes to those seen in the measured habitat parameters.

We did not conduct formal power analyses for this protocol for three reasons: (1) The primary purpose of conducting a prospective power analysis is to determine whether the proposed sample size is adequate. For most parks, we already have the maximum number of sites that will fit within the sample frame, without decreasing plot size and thus increasing the risk of double sampling individuals. (2) Most of our data analyses will take the form of parameter estimation rather than null hypothesis significance testing. When estimating parameters, there is no associated statistical power. (3) Statistical power is dependent upon the hypothesis under test and the statistical test used. Over the course of this long-term monitoring program, we could potentially evaluate a number of different hypotheses. Thus there is no single 'power' relevant to the overall protocol. Estimating power at this point in the context of such a long-term, multifaceted monitoring program could be potentially misleading. In general, statistical power analyses are frequently mis-used and misinterpreted in ecological contexts (Morrison 2007), and alternative approaches to evaluating the degree of uncertainty associated with our data will be evaluated and used when applicable.

5a. Bird Data Analysis

Prior to summary analyses, the residency status (permanent resident, summer resident, migrant) of each bird species recorded is determined. Identifying the residency of each species helps to exclude migrants from analyses of breeding birds within a park. Each time a survey is conducted the frequency and abundance of bird species is reported in four ways: 1) number of individuals in each species encountered per plot visit (individuals/plot visit); 2) proportion of plots occupied by each species (total number of plots occupied by a species/total number of plots sampled); 3) park-wide species density, and 4) localized species densities (i.e. the density of a species on plots it occupies). Initially, species density is derived from observations within a 100-m radius (3.14 ha) around each plot center. Distance software, which accounts for undetected individuals, should be used to calculate species density estimates once there are enough observations to do so accurately (Buckland et al. 1993, Buckland et al. 2001). Ideally, 60-80 detections are needed to compute a distance function for a species (Buckland et al. 1993). However, it is possible to pool data from multiple surveys over a number of years to obtain adequate sample sizes for development of these detection functions. Also, if the detectability of a particular species is high and factors affecting detection rate are not complex, it is possible to obtain adequate results with fewer than 60 detections.

Annual bird richness, diversity, and distribution evenness are calculated by plot and averaged across major habitat types (i.e. riparian, woodland, prairie, etc) or park-wide. Species richness is defined as the total number of bird species observed on a plot. A map should be created and included in a report showing species richness and the richness of species of continental importance, as determined by Partners in Flight (Rich et al. 2004). Species diversity, calculated using the Shannon Diversity Index (Shannon, 1949), measures the equitability of species observed on a plot. The disparity among species abundance is calculated using Pielou's "J" (Pielou, 1969). Both species and community diversity measures should be calculated based only on males, as this segment of the bird community is the most readily observed and presents the best opportunity to measure population changes through time.

To evaluate changes over time, a regression approach will be applied to the data. The predictor variable will be time and the response variable could be abundance of a particular species or one of the community diversity metrics. A control chart approach (Morrison 2008) could also be used to evaluate change over time and signal the need for management to act, if meaningful thresholds can be determined. These methods are discussed in detail in SOP #9.8 "Data Analysis". Multivariate control charts that consider all species in the community simultaneously may also be constructed (Anderson and Thompson 2004). This approach appears to have promise but has not been widely applied nor thoroughly evaluated, and further evaluation of this method is warranted before application to the data of this protocol.

5b. Habitat Data Analysis

Summaries of habitat attributes at the 50-m plot level are required for "permanent" and "semi-permanent" features. For permanent features, the values for slope, aspect and topographic position are measured, reported, and assigned to a permanent locations table within the database only once. Semi-permanent plot features (those not expected to change much, including percent cover of coarse habitat types, road, and water cover) are recorded each time a survey is conducted, and these changes are reported.

The bulk of habitat data is collected at the 5-m subplot level. Like permanent attributes measured on plots, permanent features for subplots (i.e. slope and aspects) are measured only once, and stored in a table within the database. Subplot features reported on each time a survey is conducted include tree tallies (stems/ha), canopy height, canopy coverage, basal area, ground and foliar coverage, horizontal vegetation coverage and structural diversity. Ground cover includes deciduous and grass litter, bare soil, rock, woody debris (>2.50 cm DBH), and unvegetated. Foliar cover, determined by guilds, includes warm- and cool-season grasses, forbs, mosses and lichens, shrubs and vines, tree seedlings and total foliar cover (<1.50 m tall).

An appendix listing habitat parameter values recorded for each plot should be included in each report. Plot specific habitat metrics in conjunction with plot specific bird data serve as a first cut in trying to understand habitat use by a species, especially those of continental importance.

To further evaluate relationships between bird metrics and habitat variables, pairwise bivariate correlations can be calculated if interest is on a single habitat variable. If multiple habitat variables are of interest, a multiple regression approach can be used. If interest focuses on the presence or absence of particular bird species, rather than their abundance or community diversity metrics, logistic regression (simple or multiple) would be appropriate. If model selection is the goal, an information theoretic approach such as Akaike's Information Criterion (AIC) will be used. These methods are discussed in detail in SOP #9.8 "Data Analysis".

5c. Reporting

To facilitate timely dissemination of monitoring results, status reports should be completed by March 31 of the year following data collection by the HTLN. More extensive summary reports should be completed every eight to twelve years depending on how fast habitat conditions are changing and how critical summary information is to setting management goals influencing bird populations within a park. Summary reports may be used in place of annual reports for that year. To the extent possible, the reporting of bird monitoring and habitat assessment results should be coordinated with the reporting of results from other HTLN projects (i.e. vegetation monitoring). All reports must follow National Park Service Natural Resource Technical Report formatting style. Refer to SOP #9.10 "Reporting" for details on report structure and style.

Tables and figures (including pictures) in a report should be placed within the text or immediately following the literature cited section. Tables and figures should be numbered in sequence regardless of where they are located. Table captions are placed at the top of a table, while figure captions are placed below the figure. Horizontal lines are used to separate the table caption from column headings, column headings from the table, and to signify the end of the table. Vertical lines should not be used in tables. Tables and figures should contain information not presented in the body of the text, thereby minimizing redundancy.

6. Personnel Requirements and Training

6a. Roles and Responsibilities

The project manager is the lead ecologist for implementing this monitoring protocol, and is supervised by the Program Coordinator for the HTLN. Because of the need for a high level of training and consistency in implementing the protocol, the project manager will usually be the person conducting the VCP counts in the field. The data management aspect of the monitoring effort is the shared responsibility of the project manager and the data manager. Typically, the project manager is responsible for data collection, data entry, data verification and validation, as well as data summary, analysis and reporting. The data manager is responsible for data archiving, data security, dissemination and database design. The data manager, in collaboration with the project manager, also develops data entry forms and other database features as part of quality assurance and automates report generation. The data manager is ultimately responsible that adequate QA/QC procedures are built into the database management system and appropriate data handling procedures followed.

6b. Qualifications and Training

The most essential component for the collection of credible, high-quality data on birds is a competent observer. This cannot be overemphasized. Various studies have shown that observer bias is one of the most noteworthy bias factors in trend analysis of songbird populations (Scott et al. 1986, Sauer et al. 1994, Kendall et al. 1996).

As well as being able to visually identify birds, field observers must be proficient at identifying species by their songs and calls. Therefore, recordings of birds in the study area, especially for the less common or unexpected species, should be provided for surveyors. Observers should be tested frequently on their ability to identify bird calls. Good hearing ability is essential because many birds, particularly in forested habitats, are detected by sound only. Differences in hearing ability between observers may strongly affect survey results (Ramsey and Scott 1981).

The quality of the observer will determine the quality of the data. Time should also be invested in training personnel to estimate the distance from themselves to singing birds within different habitats. This will require training in the field (see SOP #9.2, "Training Observers") to become proficient with the use of a laser rangefinder and to gain experience with estimating distances to different species in different habitat types.

The project manager and a staff botanist will assist in training the bird crew to conduct habitat monitoring. Habitat observers should familiarize themselves with the HTLN standard cover classes and vegetation guilds described in SOP #9.6. Prior to the field season, observers should practice estimating cover of different vegetation guilds and ground cover categories within

1.78-m radius practice plots. If habitat monitoring cannot be practiced prior to the field season, a staff botanist will accompany the bird crew on the first field trip of the year.

7. Operational Requirements

7a. Annual Workload and Field Schedule

Breeding bird surveys will begin no sooner than the first full week of May and extend no later then the second full week of June, a period that coincides with the peak-breeding activity of most birds. Inclement weather and personnel workloads will preclude the scheduling of sampling events to specific annual dates. Bird surveys may be scheduled for the third week of June if spring green-up is unusually late. Habitat monitoring should be completed no later than June 30, in order for habitat measures to accurately reflect conditions experienced by breeding birds. Monitoring efforts will require a three to four person crew. Approximately three to seven field days are required to complete bird sampling at most parks. However, 10 – 12 days should be planned for at Tallgrass Prairie National Preserve. Twelve to fifteen VCP counts should be scheduled for completion each field day.

7b. Facility and Equipment Needs

The nature of bird survey work does not require special facilities beyond normal office space and equipment storage needs. Table 1.1 is a list of field equipment needs for one crew. If two or more crews work simultaneously, equipment requirements will increase accordingly.

7c. Startup Costs and Budget Considerations

Personnel expenses for field work are based on a crew of three people: an ecologist to conduct the bird counts, a biologist to lead habitat sampling and a biological science technician to assist with habitat sampling. Field days should be planned by dividing the number of plots to be sampled that year by 15, the number of plots that can be sampled in one day, and then adding any extra travel days that may be required to accomplish the field work. Field costs will vary somewhat from year to year depending on the skill level and size of the crew. Table 7.3.1 lists an average annual cost to complete field work. Data management personnel expenses include staff time of a biological science technician, a biologist, the project manager and data manager. Equipment/supplies include funds for the purchase of equipment and supplies for bird monitoring, as well as maintenance and or replacement of equipment shared among multiple projects (e.g. GPS units, cameras).

Table 2. Estimated annual budget for bird monitoring by the Heartland Network Inventory and Monitoring Program.

Category	Costs
Staff salary	$96,037.84
Administrative support to WICR	$2593.50
Field work travel	$4,693.00
Computer hardware and software	$1,235.,00
Vehicle lease	$2,964.00
Field / office equipment	$2,223.00
Supplies	$1,482.00
Total	**$111,228.34**

7d. Procedure for Revising the Protocol

Over time, revisions to both the Protocol Narrative and to specific Standard Operating Procedures (SOPs) are to be expected. Careful documentation of changes to the protocol and a library of previous protocol versions are essential for maintaining consistency in data collection and for appropriate treatment of the data during data summary and analysis. The Microsoft Access® database for each monitoring component contains a field that identifies which version of the protocol was being used when the data were collected.

The rationale for dividing a sampling protocol into a Protocol Narrative with supporting SOPs is based on the following:

- The Protocol Narrative is a general overview of the protocol that gives the history and justification for doing the work and an overview of the sampling methods, but does not provide all the methodological details. The Protocol Narrative will only be revised if major changes are made to the protocol.

- The SOPs, in contrast, are very specific step-by-step instructions for performing a given task. They are expected to be revised more frequently than the protocol narrative.

- When a SOP is revised, in most cases, it is not necessary to revise the Protocol Narrative to reflect the specific changes made to the SOP.

- All versions of the Protocol Narrative and SOPs will be archived in a Protocol Library.

The steps for changing the protocol (either the Protocol Narrative or the SOPs) are outlined in SOP #9.11, "Revising the Protocol." Each SOP contains a Revision History Log that should be filled out each time a SOP is revised to explain why the change was made, and to assign a new Version Number to the revised SOP. The new version of the SOP and/or Protocol Narrative should then be archived in the HTLN Protocol Library under the appropriate folder.

8. References

Anderson, M.J., and A.A. Thompson. 2004. Multivariate control charts for ecological and environmental monitoring. Ecological Applications 14:1921-1935.

Barker, R. J., and J. R. Sauer. 1995. Statistical aspects of point count sampling. Pages 125-130 *in* C. J. Ralph, J. R. Sauer, and S. Droege, eds. Monitoring Bird Populations by Point Counts, USDA Forest Service, Pacific Southwest Research Station, General Technical Report PSW-GTR-149.

Bibby, C. J., N. D. Burgess, D. A. Hill, and S. Mustoe. 2000. Bird Census Techniques. Second Edition. Academic Press, London. 302 pp.

British Columbia Resource Inventory Branch (BCRIB). 1999. Inventory methods for forest and grassland songbirds: standards for components of British Columbia's biodiversity No. 15. Resource Inventory Branch, British Columbia Ministry of Environment, Lands and Parks. Available from http://www.for.gov.bc.ca/RIC/Pubs/teBioDiv/

Buckland, S. T., D. R. Anderson, K. P. Burnham, and J. L. Laake. 1993. Distance sampling: Estimating abundance of biological populations. Chapman and Hall, New York. 446 pp.

Buckland, S. T., D. R. Anderson, K. P. Burnham, J. L. Laake, D. L. Borchers, and L. Thomas. 2001. Introduction to distance sampling: estimating abundance of biological populations. Oxford University Press. 432 pp.

Burnham, K. P. 1981. Summarizing remarks: environmental influences. Studies in Avian Biology 6:324-325.

Burnham, K.P. and Anderson, D.R. 2002. Model selection and multi-model inference. New York, N. Y., Springer-Verlag.

Cabin, R.J. and R.J. Mitchell. 2000. To Bonferroni or not to Bonferroni: When and how are the questions. Bulletin of the Ecological Society of America 81:246-248.

CBE Style Manual Committee. 1994. Scientific style and format: the CBE manual for authors, editors, and publishers. 6th edition. Council of Biology Editors, Cambridge University Press, New York, New York.

Daubenmire, R.F. 1959. Canopy coverage method of vegetation analysis. Northwest Science 33:43-64.

Day, R. A. and B. Gastel. 2006. How to write and publish a scientific paper. 6th edition. Greenwood Press, Westport, CT.

DeBacker, M. D., C. C. Young, P. Adams., L. Morrison, D. Peitz, G. A. Rowell, M. Williams, and D. Bowles. 2005. Heartland Inventory and Monitoring and Prairie Cluster Prototype

Monitoring Program vital signs monitoring plan. U.S. National Park Service, Heartland I&M Network and Prairie Cluster Prototype Monitoring Program, Wilson's Creek National Battlefield, Republic, Missouri.

Fancy, S. G. 1997. A new approach for analyzing bird densities from variable circular-plot counts. Pacific Science 51:107-114.

Ford, B., S. Carr, C Hunter, J. York, and M. Roedel. 2000. Partner in Flight bird conservation plan for the Interior Low Plateaus (Physiographic Area # 14). Cornell Lab of Ornithology, Ithaca, New York. 55pp.

Goldwasser, L. 1999. A collection of grammatical points. Bulletin of the Ecological Society of America. **79**: 148-150.

Harrell, F.E. 2001. Regression modeling strategies: With applications to linear models, logistic regression, and survival analysis. New York and Berlin, Springer.

Hatfield, J.S., Gould, W.R.t., Hoover, B.A., Fuller, M.R. and Lindquist, E.L. 1996. Detecting trends in raptor counts: power and Type I error rates of various statistical tests. Wildlife Society Bulletin 24: 505-515.

Hayek, L.C. and M.A. Buzas. 1997. Surveying Natural Populations. Columbia University Press, New York, NY.

Hosmer, D.W. and Lemeshow, S. 2000. Applied logistic regression. New York, John Wiley and Sons.

Karr, J. R. 1991. Biological integrity: a long-neglected aspect of water resource management. Ecological Applications 1:66-84.

Karr, J. R. and D. R. Dudley. 1981. Ecological perspective on water quality goals. Environmental Management 5:55-68.

Kendall, W. L., B. G. Peterjohn, and J. R. Sauer. 1996. First-time observer effects in the North American Breeding Bird Survey. Auk 113:823-829.

Kepler, C. B. and J. M. Scott. 1981. Reducing bird count variability by training observers. Studies in Avian Biology 6:366-371.

Knopf, F.L. and F.B. Samson. 1997. Conservation of grassland vertebrates. Pages 273-289 *in* F.L. Knopf and F.B. Samson, eds. Ecology and Conservation of Great Plains Vertebrates. Springer-Verlag, New York, New York.

Kutner, M. H., C. J. Nachtsheim, J. Neter, and W. Li. 2005. Applied Linear Statistical Models. McGraw Hill Irwin, Boston, MA.

MacCallum, R.C., Widaman, K.F., Zhang, S. and Hong, S. 1999. Sample size in factor analysis. Psychological Methods 4: 84-99.

MacNally, R. 2000. Regression and model-building in conservation biology, biogeography and ecology: The distinction between--and reconciliation of--'predictive' and 'explanatory' models. Biodiversity and Conservation 9: 655-671.

Mack, R. N. 1986. Writing with precision, clarity, and economy. Bulletin of Ecological Society of America **67**:31-35.

Maurer, B.A. 1993. Biological diversity, ecological integrity, and neotropical migrants: New perspectives for wildlife managers. Pages 24-31 *in* D.M. Finch and P.W. Stangel, editors. Status and management of neotropical migratory birds. U.S. Forest Service General Technical Report RM-229.

Moran, M.D. 2003. Arguments for rejecting the sequential Bonferroni in ecological studies. Oikos 100:403-405.

Morrison, L.W. 2007. Assessing the reliability of ecological monitoring data: Power analysis and alternative approaches. Natural Areas Journal 27: 83-91.

Morrison, L.W. 2008. The use of control charts to interpret environmental monitoring data. Natural Areas Journal 28: 66-73.

Nakagawa, S. 2004. A farewell to Bonferroni: the problems of low statistical power and publication bias. Behavioral Ecology 15:1044-10445.

National Park Service. 2006. Inventory and Monitoring Natural Resource Database Template Version 3.1 documentation. Natural Resource Program Center, Office of Inventory, Monitoring, and Evaluation, Fort Collins, CO. 28 pp.

Nelson, J. T. and S. G. Fancy. 1999. A test of the variable circular-plot method when exact density of a bird population was known. Pacific Conservation Biology 5:139-143.

Peitz, D.G., S.G. Fancy, L.P. Thomas, G.A. Rowell, and M.D. DeBacker. 2003. Bird monitoring protocol for Agate Fossil Beds National Monument, Nebraska and Tallgrass Prairie National Preserve, Kansas. Prairie Cluster Prototype Long-term Ecological Monitoring Program, National Park Service, Department of the Interior.

Perneger, T.V. 1998. What's wrong with Bonferroni adjustments. British Medical Journal 316:1236-1238.

Pickett, S.T.A., V.T. Parker and P.T. Fiedler. 1992. The new paradigm in ecology: implications for conservation biology above the species level. Pages 65-88 in P.L. Fiedler and S.K. Jain (editors) Conservation Biology: The Theory and Practice of Conservation, Preservation and Management. Chapman and Hall, New York, New York. 507pp.

Powell, A. N. 2000. Grassland bird inventory of seven prairie parks. Final report to the Great Plains Prairie Cluster Long-term Ecological Monitoring Program, Wilson's Creek National Battlefield, National Park Service, U.S. Department of the Interior, Republic, Missouri. 47 p.

Pielou, E.C. 1969. An introduction to mathematical ecology. John Wiley and Sons, New York, New York. 286pp.

Pielou, E.C. 1977. Population and Community Ecology. New York: Gordon and Breach.

Ralph, C. J., G. R. Geupel, P. Pyle, T. E. Martin and D. F. DeSante. 1993. Handbook of field methods for monitoring landbirds. USDA Forest Service, Pacific Southwest Research Station, General Technical Report PSW-GTR-144

Ralph, C. J., S. Droege, and J. R. Sauer. 1995. Managing and monitoring birds using point counts: standards and applications. Pages 161-168 *in* C. J. Ralph, J. R. Sauer, and S. Droege, eds. Monitoring Bird Populations by Point Counts, USDA Forest Service, Pacific Southwest Research Station, General Technical Report PSW-GTR-149.

Ramsey, F. L. and J. M. Scott. 1981. Tests of hearing ability. Studies in Avian Biology 6:341-345.

Reynolds, R. T., J. M. Scott, and R. A. Nussbaum. 1980. A variable circular-plot method for estimating bird numbers. Condor 82:309-313.

Rice, W.R. 1989. Analyzing tables of statistical tests. Evolution 43:223-225.

Rich, T.D., C.J. Beardmore, H. Berlanga, P.J. Blancher, M.S.W. Bradstreet, G.S. Butcher, D.W. Demarest, E.H. Dunn, W.C. Hunter, E.E. Inigo-Elias, J.A. Kennedy, A.M. Martell. A.O. Panjabi, D.N. Pashley, K.V. Rosenberg, C.M. Rustay, J.S. Wendt, T.C. Will. 2004. Partners in Flight North American landbird conservation plan. Cornell Lab of Ornithology, Ithaca, New York. 84pp.

Roman, S. 2002. Access Database: Design and Programming. O'Reilly Media. Sebastapol, Ca.

Rowell, G.A., M. H. Williams, and M. D. DeBacker. 2005. Data Management Plan: Heartland I&M Network and Prairie Cluster Prototype Monitoring Program. Wilson's Creek National Battlefield, Republic, Missouri. 64pp.

Rowell, G.A. and M.H. Williams. 2007. Standard Operating Procedure: WICR Heartland Network System Backups. Heartland Inventory and Monitoring Network. Wilson's Creek National Battlefield, Republic, Missouri.

Sauer, J. R., B. G. Peterjohn, and W. A. Link. 1994. Observer differences in the North American Breeding Bird Survey. Auk 111:50-62.

Sauer, J. R., J. E. Hines, I. Thomas, J. Fallon, and G. Gough. 2000. The North American breeding bird survey, results and analysis 1966 – 1999. Version 98.1, USGS Patuxent Wildlife Research Center, Laurel, Maryland. Available at http://www.mbr-pwrc.usgs.gov/bbs/bbs.html

Sauer, J. R., J. E. Hines, and J. Fallon. 2003. The North American breeding bird survey, results and analysis 1966 - 2002. Version 2003.1, USGS Patuxent Wildlife Research Center, Laurel, Maryland. Available at http://www.mbr-pwrc.usgs.gov/bbs/bbs.html

Scott, J. M., S. Mountainspring, F. L. Ramsey, and C. B. Kepler. 1986. Forest bird communities of the Hawaiian Islands: Their dynamics, ecology and conservation. Studies in Avian Biology 9:1-431.

Shannon, C.E. 1949. The mathematical theory of communication. University of Illinois Press, Urbana, Illinois. 177 pp.

Smith, W.B., P.D. Miles, J.S. Vissage and S.A. Pugh. 2004. Forest resources of the United States, 2002. General Technical Report NC-241. North Central Research Station, Forest Service, U.S. Department of Agriculture, St Paul, Minnesota. 137 pp.

Strunk, W., Jr., and E. B. White. 2000. The Elements of Style. 4th Edition. Macmillan, New York, New York.

Thomas, L. 1996. Monitoring long-term population change: Why are there so many analysis methods? Ecology 77: 49-58.

Twedt, D.J., D.N. Pashley, W.C. Hunter, A.J. Mueller, C. Brown and R.P. Ford. 1999. Partners in Flight bird conservation plan for the Mississippi Alluvial Valley (Physiographic Area # 05). Cornell Lab of Ornithology, Ithaca, New York. 46pp.

Whittingham, M.J., Stephens, P.A., Bradbury, R.B. and Freckleton, R.P. 2006. Why do we still use stepwise modelling in ecology and behaviour? Journal of Animal Ecology 75: 1182-1189.

9. Standard Operating Procedures

Breeding Bird Monitoring Protocol for the Heartland Network Inventory and Monitoring Program

Standard Operation Procedure 1: Preparations & Equipment Setup Prior to Field Season

Version 2.00 (05/09/2008)

Revision History Log:

Previous Version #	Revision Date	Author	Changes Made	Reason for Change	New Version #
1.00	Jun. 2004	D.G. Peitz	Edited wording page 2	Edited to reflect changes in the annual sampling effort at TAPR	1.01

Prior to the field season each year, usually beginning in March or April, all observers should review this entire protocol, including SOPs. Review of bird identification by sight and sound (SOP #9.2 "Training Observers") is particularly important; misidentification of a species is perhaps the most serious error you can make during a bird count. Misidentification is much more serious than errors in estimating distances or double-counting a bird. This SOP also gives a brief description of how bird monitoring should be scheduled. Preseason planning facilitates the completion of both bird surveys and habitat work. All observers should follow the outlined field schedule to avoid double sampling of plots or initiating habitat work on a plot prior to it being sampled for birds. All of the equipment and supplies listed in this SOP should be organized and made ready for the field season, and copies of the field data forms in SOP #9.5 "Conducting the Variable Circular Plot Count" and SOP #9.6 "Documenting Habitat Variables" should be made. Approximately twenty-five percent of the field data forms should be copied to write-in-the-rain paper.

I. General Preparation and Review

1. Notebooks from previous surveys should be reviewed if available to identify any unique events that may be encountered. A field notebook for the survey year should be prepared with pages for entry of sampling schedules, observer names, field hours and unique happenings that may influence how the data are reported. Trip reports are based on information recorded in field notebooks so it is imperative that they are clearly organized for ease of field note entry.

2. Prior knowledge of species most likely to be encountered in a park will aid birders in preparing for the birding season. Therefore, species lists from previous birding efforts in a park or local area should be compiled and compared to reference manuals to identify species not recorded which have a probability of being recorded. Copies of these combined species list should be carried into the field as quick references in helping to identify unknown birds. Appendix C lists avian species most likely to be encountered during the breeding season, by park.

3. Waypoints for each variable circular plot (VCP) must be loaded onto the GPS unit prior to the start of the field season. Waypoints are the X and Y coordinates for each VCP and are used to navigate to their location. Appendix B contains lists of VCP locations with their associated UTM coordinates by park. Way points for bird plots are stored on the HTLN server computer under the grassland bird project folder at L:\HTLN\Projects\HtlnWicr\GrasslandBirds\SpatialInfo\Waypoints, by park.

II. Scheduling Field Work

1. Breeding bird surveys will begin no sooner than the first full week of May and extend no later then the second full week of June, a period that coincides with the peak breeding activity of most birds. Inclement weather and personnel workloads will preclude the scheduling of sampling events to specific annual dates. Sampling dates should be scheduled and logistics organized prior to the start of each field season. Completion of habitat monitoring needs to be scheduled for no later than June 30; changing habitat conditions due to plant growth and large ungulate grazing (where permitted) requires this to correlate bird populations with habitat type.

2. Twelve to fifteen VCP should be scheduled for completion each field day. Determine which plots will be sampled for habitat measures based on the order they will be sampled for birds. Habitat sampling should only be done on plots already sampled for birds or after the morning survey is completed to avoid disturbing birds on plots not yet sampled.

3. Habitat sampling will start as soon as the first bird plot for that day has been completed. Observers should stay back from the plot as not to disturb birds. However, they should have a sense of where the birder is and when he/she will be done surveying the plot. Two-way radios work well to communicate when a plot is ready for habitat sampling. A minimum of two people will start the habitat work, with the birder joining them after that day's survey is done.

III. Organizing Supplies and Equipment

An equipment list should be compiled, and equipment organized and made ready for the field season several weeks in advance of the field season. This allows time to make needed repairs and order equipment. The following is a list of field equipment needs for one crew, if two or more crews work simultaneously equipment needs will change accordingly.

Table 1.1. Field equipment list for variable circular plot bird counts and habitat work.

Number Req.	Description
	Bird surveys
1	HTLN bird identification reference book with species separated by parks
1	10 x 50 or better binoculars
1	Rangefinder (1000 yd. range or better)
1	Tape recorder for recording unknown bird calls
1	Celsius thermometer
1	GPS unit and accompanying SOP for navigating to bird plots
50 – 100	36-in. pin flags with 4 x 5 in. flag (florescent pink works well)
2 – 3	Sharpie or other permanent marker for marking plot numbers on pin flags
	Habitat work
1	5.0-m rope with attached surveying pin to mark subplot boundaries
1	1.78-m rope with attached surveying pin to mark sampling plot boundaries
8	Surveyors pin for delineating the bounds of the 1.78-m sampling plots
2	1.27-cm x 1-m PVC pipe for measuring slope
1	English clinometer for measuring slope
1	Metric clinometer for measuring tree height
1	Densiometer for measuring canopy cover
1	Cruz-all (10 factor English) or Prizm (2.5 factor metric)
1	0.15 x 2.0-m horizontal structure board
1	7.5-m telescoping graduated measuring rod for measuring vertical structure
1	5-m D-tape for measuring tree diameters
2	50-m tapes (100-m tape may by substituted for one 50-m tape)
	Both elements of bird monitoring
2	Compass for direction between plots and plot and subplot aspects
2	Clip boards for recording data and carrying data sheet
2 – 3	Cruising vest for carrying equipment (backpack and hip packs may be substituted)
2	Two-way radios for communication between birder and habitat crew
Several	Reference books for bird and plant identification
Several	Insect repellent
Several	Sunscreen
1	First Aid kit

Suggested reference manuals for bird surveys and habitat work:

- National Geographic. 1987. Field Guide to Birds of North America, 3rd Edition. National Geographic, Washington, D.C. 480 pages.
- Robbins, C.S., B. Bruun, and H.S. Zim. 1983. Golden: A Guide to Field Identification of North American Birds. Western Publishing Company, Inc., Racine, WI. 360 pages.
- Stokes, D. W. and L. Q. Stokes. 1995. Stokes Field Guide to Birds: Western Region. Little, Brown and Company, New York, NY. 519 pages.
- Stokes, D. W. and L. Q. Stokes. 1995. Stokes Field Guide to Birds: Eastern Region. Little, Brown and Company, New York, NY. 471 pages.
- Dorm, R. D. 1992. Vascular Plants of Wyoming. Mountain West Publishing, Cheyenne, WY. 340 pages.

- Hitchcock, A. S. 1971. Manual of the Grasses of the United States (volumes I-II), 2nd edition revised by A. Chase. Dover Publications, Inc., New York, NY. 1051 pages.
- Stubbendieck J. and E. C. Conard. Common Legumes of the Great Plains: an illustrated guide. University of Nebraska Press, Lincoln, NE. 330 pages.
- Stubbendieck J., S. L. Hatch and C. H. Butterfield. 1992. North American Range Plants: 4th edition. University of Nebraska Press, Lincoln, NE. 493 pages.
- Great Plains Flora Association. 1986. Flora of the Great Plains. University Press of Kansas, Lawrence, KS. 1402 pages.
- Bare, J. E. 1979. Wildflowers and Weeds of Kansas. The Regents Press of Kansas, Lawrence, KS. 509 pages.
- HTLN reference book "Birds of ARPO, EFMO, GWCA, HEHO, HOCU, HOME, LIBO, PERI, PIPE, TAPR, WICR".
- HTLN reference book "Trees of-- ARPO, EFMO, GWCA, HEHO, HOCU, HOME, LIBO, PERI, PIPE, TAPR, and WICR".

Breeding Bird Monitoring Protocol for the Heartland Network Inventory and Monitoring Program

Standard Operation Procedure 2: Training Observers

Version 2.00 (05/09/2008)

Revision History Log:

Previous Version #	Revision Date	Author	Changes Made	Reason for Change	New Version #

This Standard Operating Procedure explains the training procedures that all observers should follow to learn: (1) how to identify birds by sight and vocalizations; (2) how to estimate distances in the field; and (3) how to estimate ground cover and measure tree characteristics.

I. Identification of Birds by Sight and Vocalizations

The most essential component for the collection of credible, high-quality bird data is well-trained and experienced observers. This cannot be overemphasized. Proficient bird observers obtain species estimates within 90% of total species known to be present and estimate abundance within 80% accuracy (Ralph et al. 1993). Various studies have shown that observer bias is one of the most noteworthy bias factors in trend analysis of songbird populations (Kepler and Scott 1981, Baker and Sauer 1995). Before conducting variable circular plot (VCP) counts, read "Reducing Bird Count Variability by Training Observers" by Kepler and Scott (1981) for a detailed discussion of training observers to identify birds by sight and sound as well as training them to estimate distances.

1. See Appendix C for a list of bird species likely to be encountered at parks within the Heartland Network Inventory and Monitoring Program (HTLN). Beginning several months prior to the field-season, review and practice bird identification skills.

2. Birders should pass a minimum proficiency test on the vocalizations and sight ID of bird species likely to be encountered, correctly identifying all common species likely to be encountered and 90% of the less frequently encountered species (i.e. species encountered less than ten times annually).

3. Regardless of skill level, birders should spend time in the field familiarizing themselves with the birds in a park prior to starting a survey.

4. Suggested reference materials for conducting bird surveys for the HTLN:

- Tapes or CDs of bird songs for species found in Arkansas, Indiana, Iowa, Kansas, Minnesota, Missouri, Ohio and Nebraska. These tapes and CDs are produced by Cornell Laboratory of Ornithology's Library of Natural Sounds and may be obtained from State Wildlife Agencies.
- National Audubon Society Interactive CD-ROM Guide to North American Birds. This interactive CD-ROM is an excellent resource for learning calls, site ID and background information on bird species.
- Bird slides of species likely to be encountered can be obtained from Cornell Laboratory of Ornithology.
- National Geographic. 1987. Field Guide to Birds of North America, 3rd Edition. National Geographic, Washington, D.C. 480 pages.
- Robbins, C.S., B. Bruun, and H.S. Zim. 1983. Golden: A Guide to Field Identification of North American Birds. Western Publishing Company, Inc., Racine, WI. 360 pages.
- Stokes, D. W. and L. Q. Stokes. 1995. Stokes Field Guide to Birds: Western Region. Little, Brown and Company, New York, NY. 519 pages.
- Stokes, D. W. and L. Q. Stokes. 1995. Stokes Field Guide to Birds: Eastern Region. Little, Brown and Company, New York, NY. 471 pages.

II. Estimating Distances to Birds Seen or Heard

Read the paper "Reducing Bird Count Variability by Training Observers" by Kepler and Scott (1981) for a detailed discussion of training observers to identify birds by sight and sound as well as training them in distance estimating. For observers who are already competent at identifying birds by sight and sound, one full day of training is usually all that is necessary to be able to estimate distances within ±10%. Experienced observers usually recalibrate themselves the afternoon before a bird survey begins (VCP counts are done early in the morning, so people usually travel to the study site on the morning before the count and recalibrate the afternoon before the count).

1. Begin by placing flagging at 10 m, 25 m, 50 m and 100 m from a central point and having observers estimate distances to trees, rocks and flagging from the central point.

2. Have each observer place flagging at 4-5 locations visible from the station, and then have everyone in the group record distances to each flag in a field book. Distances should be estimated to the nearest meter. Then, use tape measures to measure the distance to each flag, and have each person compare their initial estimate to the actual distance. A laser rangefinder may also be useful for measuring the actual distances. Repeat this exercise at several sites with both open and closed vegetation until observers can consistently estimate distances to within 10-15% of the actual distance. For objects within 20 m of the station, observers should be able to accurately estimate distances to within 1 m of the true distance.

3. The majority of birds are usually heard but not seen, and estimating distances to birds that are only heard is often the greatest source of error in VCP counts. With all observers at the central point, have each observer estimate the distance to vocalizing birds pointed out by the leader. Horizontal distances should be estimated, as if a plumb bob was lowered to the ground from the bird's location. Observers should visually identify the tree or branch where they think the bird is, and estimate the horizontal distance to an object that they can see directly below a point from where they think the bird is vocalizing.

4. Half of the group should place themselves at various distances away from the central point, and quietly wait until a bird vocalizes near them. Place reference markers at measured distances from the central point to help these "spotters" estimate the distance between the central point and birds that vocalize. The other half of the group should remain at the central point, and estimate the distance to any birds that vocalize. The observer closest to the bird should then indicate where the bird was vocalizing and if necessary, the distance to the point directly under the bird should be measured from the station using a tape measure. This is a slow but important part of the training, and should be repeated until observers have experience with estimating distances to a number of different species and call or song types.

5. Simultaneous counts: Divide observers into groups of 4-5 persons and conduct 5-minute counts from the same location. At the end of each count, have the observers compare notes and discuss any discrepancies in the species detected and the estimated distances to them. Remember that the distance to where the bird was first detected should be recorded, so that if a bird flies towards the central point, the distance where it was first heard or seen is recorded, not the closest distance or where it lands. Continue these simultaneous counts until there are consistency among observers in species and distances recorded (recommend no difference in species identification and less than 10% difference in distance estimates).

III. Collecting Habitat Data

1. Familiarize yourself with the HTLN standard cover classes, SOP #9.6 "Documenting Habitat Variables".

2. Spend time prior to the field season practicing estimating cover classes of different vegetation guilds and ground cover categories within 1.78-m practice plots. Someone skilled in conducting cover class estimates needs to assist in training and confirm cover class estimates.

3. If habitat monitoring cannot be practiced prior to the field season, than someone skilled in conducting cover class estimates must assist in collecting habitat data if consistency across years is to be maintained. However, other members on the habitat crew should be trained and proficient in estimating cover classes within the first week of conducting fieldwork.

4. Someone skilled in estimating tree heights, canopy cover and basal areas of trees influencing bird plots is also needed on the habitat crew. Instructions for using a clinometer (tree height), densiometer (canopy cover) and cruz-all or prizm (basal area) accompany each instrument and should be reviewed prior to, and followed, during field data collection. All members on the habitat crew should be trained and proficient in using each instrument within a half day of training and conducting fieldwork.

Breeding Bird Monitoring Protocol for the Heartland Network Inventory and Monitoring Program

Standard Operation Procedure 3: Using the Global Positioning System

Please see: http://science.nature.nps.gov/im/units/htln/datamanagement.cfm.

Also, the most current SOP for each GPS unit accompanies the unit into the field.

Breeding Bird Monitoring Protocol for the Heartland Network Inventory and Monitoring Program

Standard Operation Procedure 4: Establishing and Marking Sampling Plots

Version 2.00 (05/09/2008)

Revision History Log:

Previous Version #	Revision Date	Author	Changes Made	Reason for Change	New Version #
1.00	Jun. 2004	D.G. Peitz	Add sample year column to Table 4.01.1	Edited to reflect changes in the annual sampling effort at TAPR	1.01
1.01	May 2008	D.G. Peitz	Entire document	Edited to reflect that bird monitoring has been expanded to ten additional network parks	2.00

This Standard Operating Procedure explains the procedure for establishing and marking sampling plots that all observers should follow when locating survey points or adding new points in network parks.

I. Procedures:

1. Permanent sampling locations or 'plots' were selected by overlaying a systematic grid (originating from a random start point) on a park map (Appendix A). Systematic sampling across a park allows us to make park-wide inferences concerning the avian community. Grid size varied by park based on the size of the unit (Table 4.1). By increasing the number of sites at which bird observations are made on small parks, we increase the likelihood that rare birds present at the park will be observed. Using smaller grids in smaller park units also increases the overall number of bird observations, thus more accurate estimates of abundance for all species can be made. This is advantageous, as many birds are uncommon or cryptic and may be represented by only one or few sightings (or not seen at all in some years), making it difficult to interpret situations where one individual was present in year one, but none in year two. At large parks, the number of sampling locations is not an issue, and sampling the number of plots generated by smaller grids would be cost prohibitive. The orientation of the systematic grid was rotated from north 45 degrees at: Arkansas Post National Memorial, Arkansas (ARPO); George Washington Carver National Monument, Missouri (GWCA); Homestead

National Monument of America, Nebraska (HOME); Lincoln Boyhood National Memorial, Indiana (LIBO); Pea Ridge National Military Park, Arkansas (PERI); Pipestone National Monument, Minnesota (PIPE); and Wilson's Creek National Battlefield, Missouri (WICR) to prevent sampling sites from being influenced by man-made features (roads, fences, etc.) oriented along cardinal directions. The systematic grid at Effigy Mounds National Monument (EFMO) and Herbert Hoover National Historic Site (HEHO), Iowa were rotated from north 8 and 52 degrees, respectively, to match existing vegetation grids. The angle of the sampling grid at Tallgrass Prairie National Preserve (TAPR), Kansas was selected randomly and equals 34 degrees from north. The unique shapes of the different units at Hopewell Culture National Historical Site (HOCU), Ohio dictated that the systematic grid be oriented in cardinal directions.

Table 4.1. Sample grid sizes for parks in the Heartland Network Inventory and Monitoring Program.

Park	Grid size
Arkansas Post National Memorial, Arkansas	200 m x 200 m
Effigy Mounds National Monument, Iowa	400 m x 400 m
George Washington Carver National Monument, Missouri	100 m x 100 m
Herbert Hoover National Historic Site, Iowa	100 m x 100 m
Hopewell Culture National Historical Site, Ohio	400 m x 400 m
Homestead National Monument of America, Nebraska	100 m x 100 m
Lincoln Boyhood National Memorial, Indiana	100 m x 100 m
Pea Ridge National Military Park, Arkansas	400 m x 400 m
Pipestone National Monument, Minnesota	100 m x 100 m
Tallgrass Prairie National Preserve, Kansas	400 m x 400 m
Wilson's Creek National Battlefield, Missouri	400 m x 400 m

2. At TAPR, the riparian corridor was identified as a separate stratum, with sampling extending 125 m on either side of the stream channel (Palmer and Fox Creeks). The riparian stratum makes up 5.3% of the total park area (4398 ha) at TAPR. Within the riparian stratum, plots were located at 250 m intervals along the extent of the stream. Plots were placed 10 m south of the stream channel on west-east flowing streams (Palmer Creek) and 10 m west of north-south flowing streams (Fox Creek). Any plots from the overall park grid that fell within the riparian stratum were discarded.

This site selection approach allows flexibility to choose the appropriate reference frame to answer different monitoring questions. When making park-wide inferences, estimates for the two strata will be combined according to each strata's proportionate area contribution to give an overall park mean and variance. At the same time, more intensive sampling in the riparian corridor will ensure an adequate sample to describe habitat relationships specific to this less common, but important stratum. The systematic grid will also allow us to limit the reference frame appropriately when asking more specific monitoring questions (e.g. only those sampling points within particular management units would be used to compare the avian response to different fire or grazing regimes).

3. During bird surveys, sampling points are located using a GPS unit and temporarily marked with 36-in pin flags to aid in re-locating the point for habitat assessment. Warning: grazing ungulates sometimes eat pin flags, a problem that increases with time between the bird survey and habitat work on a plot. Pin flags are collected from a plot once the habitat work for that plot is completed. Each year, the sampling points are located again using a GPS unit, eliminating the need for permanent marking of each point.

4. Park maps indicating plot locations and plot ID numbers are printed prior to the start of the field season to assist in tracking completion of the work and navigating from point to point. Parks maps with bird point locations are included in Appendix A.

5. All UTM coordinates (way-points) should be entered into the GPS unit prior to the start of the field season. The appropriate UTM zones and UTM coordinates for all survey points at each HTLN park are included in Appendix B.

Breeding Bird Monitoring Protocol for the Heartland Network Inventory and Monitoring Program

Standard Operation Procedure 5: Conducting the Variable Circular Plot Count

Version 2.00 (05/09/2008)

Revision History Log:

Previous Version #	Revision Date	Author	Changes Made	Reason for Change	New Version #

This SOP gives step-by-step instructions for conducting 5-minute bird counts at parks within the Heartland Network Inventory and Monitoring Program (HTLN) using the variable circular plot (VCP) methodology. The SOP describes the procedure for collecting data and filling in the data form "Field Data Form – Variable Circular Plot Counts" (Form 1).

I. Procedures

1. Prior to the day of the counts, determine which plots will be sampled in which order, and make a list that will be taken into the field of the UTMX and UTMY coordinates for those plots.

2. Sampling will occur in the morning, beginning as soon as it is light enough to see a distance of at least 200 m and ending no later than 4 hours after official sunrise. Try to arrive at the first plot while it is still dark so that the count can begin as soon as it is light enough to see. Singing rate for most species is usually highest before or near official sunrise and then declines slowly for the next four hours.

3. Do not conduct the count during high winds or heavy rains because these conditions inhibit bird activity and impair your ability to see and hear birds. Counts should not be conducted if wind strength on the Beaufort Scale is a sustained 4 or greater (see Table 5.1), or if it is raining hard or snowing (rain code >4 in Table 5.2). If you encounter these conditions, wait until the weather improves or else cancel the sampling for that day and try again on another day.

4. Navigate to the coordinates of each plot on the list using the GPS. Approach the plot vigilantly, and if you observe a bird close to the center of the plot that flushes as a result of approaching the plot, record the initial distance from the plot center to that bird on the data form. The reason for this is that a critical assumption of the distance methodology is that any bird directly at (or very close to, e.g., <5-10 m) the plot center will always be

detected, i.e., g(0) = 1. If the data are analyzed as grouped data (as recommended), this is not a problem if the bird does not move beyond the first grouping interval. However, if a bird that otherwise would have been recorded in the plot during the count flushes prior to the beginning of the count as a result of the approach of the observer, abundance will be underestimated for that species. The alternative approach is to wait for several minutes after reaching the plot before starting the count, but this approach is likely to underestimate bird density near the plot because of birds flushing as the observer approaches.

5. Once you arrive at the plot center, begin the count as soon as possible. You should have time to fill in the location, event, and weather conditions information at the top of the form during the count. If not, these can be filled in at the end of the 5-minute count.

6. Set your watch to beep at 3 minutes, and then begin the count. Once you reach the 3-minute mark, make a mark on the VCP data form and continue the count for another 2 minutes, making sure that you fill in 3-5 in the Time Interval column for any species detected between 3 and 5 minutes. Only new birds should be recorded.

7. Use a new copy of the "Field Data Form – Variable Circular Plot Counts" for each 5-minute count. Even if no birds are detected at a particular plot, there should still be a form for that plot each time it is sampled (with the first line on the form filled in as explained below under the Species code). As soon as you are able during or just after the 5-minute count, record the following information at the top of the form:

Location ID: This is the Location Identification code stored in the VCP database to refer to a particular place on the ground (the plot ID code). If you do not know what the LocationID is for this particular plot, or if you are establishing a new plot, you can instead record the 4-character ParkCode (i.e. ARPO, HEHO, TAPR, etc.) and the Location Description, such as "TAPR Plot #46". The LocationID usually contains the 4-character ParkCode, 6-character Project Code ("Tweety") and a plot number assigned by the Project Manager. An example is ARPOTweety11 for Plot Number 11 at Arkansas Post National Memorial.

Park: Record the appropriate ParkCode (i.e. ARPO, HEHO, TAPR, etc.) if you do not know the LocationID for this plot and you are going to instead write in a Location Description as described below.

Location Description: This is a brief description (<200 characters) of the sampling location referred to by the LocationID code. An example would be "TAPR Plot #46", but it could also be something like "Bird VCP plot number 46, 150 m north of highway marker 46 next to rock wall". If the LocationID for the plot is already known, you do not need to record anything in this space because a description is already stored in the database.

Survey: This is the month (spelled out) surveys were started in a park for the year listed. Examples are May 2007 and June 2008.

Date (mm/dd/yyyy): Write in the month (2 digits), day (2 digits) and year (4 digits) in the format shown. Include the forward slash. Examples are 05/02/2001 and 06/01/2001.

Starting time (hhmm): Write in the time to the nearest minute when the 5-minute counting period begins, using the hour and minute format shown. Use military time (add 12 to the hour beginning with 1 pm through 11 pm). Fill in all four digits. Examples are 0630 (6:30 am), 0802 (8:02 am). Bird sampling should not occur during the afternoon, but for the habitat form you would record 1:30 pm as 1330 and 8:00 pm would be 2000.

Observer Initials: Fill in the three initials of the person conducting the counts using capital letters. If you do not have a middle name, either make one up or put an underscore for your middle initial. Examples would be DGP for David G. Peitz or SGF for Steven G. Fancy. In the database, these initials will correspond to the full name and contact information for that person. (The 3-character initials in the database must be unique, and if two people have the same initials, one should be given an honorary middle name).

Temperature (C°): Record the ambient temperature during the 5-minute count in degrees Celsius, to one decimal place or rounded off to the nearest degree.

Wind (0-6): Record the wind code (0 through 6) from the following Table 5.1 as it applies to the strength of the wind during the 5-min count. Record the average wind condition during the 5 minutes, not the maximum condition (do not worry about gusts).

Table 5.1. Codes (Beaufort scale) used to record wind strength during bird counts.

Wind Code	Explanation
0	calm, smoke rises vertically (< 2 km/h)
1	smoke drifts (2-5 km/h)
2	light breeze felt on face, leaves rustle (6-12 km/h)
3	leaves and twigs in constant motion (13-19 km/h)
4	small branches move, raises loose paper, dust rises (20-29 km/h)
5	fresh breeze, small trees sway (30-39 km/h)
6	strong breeze, large branches moving, wind whistling (40-50 km/h)

Rain (0-5): Record the rain code (0 through 5) from the following Table 5.2 as it applies to conditions during the 5-min count.

Table 5.2. Codes used to record precipitation during bird counts.

Rain Code	Explanation
0	no rain
1	mist or fog
2	light drizzle
3	light rain
4	heavy rain; difficult to hear birds
5	Snow

Clouds (0-100): Record percent cloud cover, rounded off to the nearest 10 percent. This should be a number between 0 (no clouds) and 100 (complete overcast). If there are patches of clouds in different areas of the sky, try to image gathering all of them together into one part of the sky and recording what percent of cloud cover that would represent. Cloud cover is recorded because it affects bird activity and singing for many species.

Noise (0-3): Record the Noise Code (0-3) from the following Table 5.3 that applies to background noise conditions during the count, as it relates to your ability to hear birds.

Table 5.3. Codes used to record level of background noise as it effects observer's ability to hear birds.

Noise Code	Explanation
0	quiet; normal background noises; no interference
1	low noise; might be missing some high-pitched songs/calls of distant birds
2	medium noise; detection radius is probably substantially reduced
3	high noise; probably detecting only the loudest/closest birds

Protocol Version: Record the version and date that version was released for the protocol that was followed during bird surveys. Example: "1.01 June 2004" indicates that the version of the bird protocol that was followed was 1.01 released June 2004.

8. Once you have started your watch and begun the 5-minute counting period, record all birds heard or seen during the 5 minutes, regardless of their distance from the center of the plot. For flyovers (birds that fly above the top of the vegetation canopy, never touch down in your field of view, and do not appear to be foraging, displaying, or behaving in any other way that might suggest a link to the habitat below them) you do not need to estimate the distance to the bird; instead just enter the species code and the number of them that you detected as shown in the example below.

9. The distance that you record should be the horizontal distance in meters between the center of the plot (where you should be standing) and the location where you first detected the bird. If the bird is flying directly at you and then lands nearby, record the distance to where you first saw it flying towards you, not the distance to where it landed. For species that occur in clusters or flocks, record the distance from the observer to the center of the flock, plus the flock size. If a bird is high in a tree, image dropping a plumb bob from the bird down to the ground, and measure the distance to that spot on the ground (the horizontal distance).

10. Many birds are heard but not seen. To estimate the distance to a bird that you detect only by sound, you should first try to determine where it is and select some object near the bird, such as a tree or rock that you think it is concealed by, and then estimate the distance to that object.

11. For each bird heard or seen (at any distance) during the 5-minute counting period, record the following information on the "Field Data Form – Variable Circular Plot Counts":

Time Interval: Enter either 0-3 or 3-5, depending on whether you first detected this bird (or flock) during the first 3 minutes of the count or during the last 2 minutes of the 5-minute count. This approach makes it possible to compare the data to those collected during BBS counts, which involve a 3-minute sampling period, by analyzing only birds detected during the first 3 minutes of the VCP count, and only those birds detected with 400 meters of the observer (the cutoff distance for BBS counts).

Observ. # (Observation Number): This is an observation number that will help tie records in the database back to the paper copy of the field data form. Each row on the data form will be given a number (1, 2, 3, 4, etc.). The numbers do not need to be sequential, so if you make a mistake and delete a row from the data sheet, it does not matter that there is a gap in the observation numbers.

Species: This is the 4-character AOU code for the species detected. Examples are WEME for Western Meadowlark, CCLO for Chestnut-collared Longspur and BHGR for Black-headed Grosbeak. These codes are usually easy to determine based on a bird's AOU common name, except where more than one species has the same code and one has to be modified from the convention. Codes for species known to occur at parks in the HTLN are listed in Appendix A of the protocol. If no birds are detected during a 5-minute count, you should enter data for the first line of the form (0-3 for Time Interval and 1 for Observ. #) and record the code NOBI for "No Birds" in the Species column.

Distance (m): Record the horizontal distance in meters between the center of the plot where you are standing, and the location or presumed location of the bird where you first detected it. Use a laser range-finder whenever possible to get as accurate a distance as possible. Do not round off numbers to the nearest 5 m; estimate the distance to the nearest meter. If you cannot see the bird, estimate the distance to some object (tree, bush, rock) where you think the bird is located.

DT (Detection Type): Record a number (1, 2, 4, 8 or 9) for the detection type based on the following explanations:
    1 = heard first, but not seen (i.e., detected initially by sound) during the 5-minute count
    2 = seen first (regardless of whether it was later heard or not) during the 5-minute count
    4 = heard first, but then seen (a DT of 1 can be changed to a 4) during the 5-minute count

Two additional Detection Type codes can be used for birds that are not detected during the 5-minute count, but that are detected while traveling between plots or before or after the 5-minute sampling period begins. These data are useful for developing annual checklists of birds occurring in the park and for distribution information.

      8 = heard, but not during the 5-minute sampling period

      9 = seen, but not during the 5-minute sampling period

The Detection Type code will be used later in various analyses. For example, distances to birds that are seen (code 2 or 4) are probably more accurate than those to birds that are only heard (DT = 1). Recording the DT makes it possible to develop distance histograms to compare birds seen versus those that are only heard. Also, there are probably different detection functions for birds heard versus seen, and recording the DT makes it possible to analyze data separately if needed.

Sex: Record the sex (Male, Female, Unknown) of the bird whenever possible. If it is known that only males of a species sing, and a bird is detected only by song, record the sex as Male.

Age: Record the age category (Adult, Juvenile, Unknown) of the bird whenever possible.

Flock Size: For most species, each individual bird will be treated independently as a separate observation, but for species that usually occur in clusters or flocks, the appropriate unit is the cluster or flock, and not the individual bird. For example, if quail almost always occur in coveys of 10 to 40 birds, and you observe a covey of 40 quail during a count, it is not appropriate to record 40 distances and treat them as independent observations in the analysis. For flocking species, record the distance to the center of the flock and the number of birds in the flock, rather than the distance to each individual bird.

Prev. Plot (Previous Plot): Place an X in this column if the bird was already detected from a previous plot. Bias caused by repeated counting of the same individual from more than one plot is usually small unless repeated counting is common during a survey (Buckland et al. 1993:37) or in cases where a rare bird is counted from multiple plots (Nelson and Fancy 1999). Recording whether a bird is thought to have been counted at a previous plot allows the data to be analyzed two different ways, depending on which is most appropriate. Some authorities say that you should not count a bird if you think it was recorded from another plot already, whereas other authorities argue that you should always count each bird detected, even if it was probably detected previously. By placing an X in this column for those cases where you think the bird has already been counted from another station, you allow future investigators the option of analyzing data by either approach.

Flyover (Number of Flyovers): Use the flyover column to record the number of birds of a particular species that fly above the top of the vegetation canopy, never touch down in your field of view, and do not appear to be foraging, displaying, or behaving in any other way that might suggest a link to the habitat below them. These are birds that appear to just be passing over, without actually utilizing the habitat you are surveying. Do not

estimate distance to these birds; instead just enter the number of them that you detected, as shown in the example below.

Comments: Record any comments that seem appropriate and that might help someone interpret and analyze the data correctly.

At the end of the day, compare vocalizations with known bird sounds on tapes to identify all unknown bird species recorded in the field. If a species is seen in the field and characteristics recorded but it was not identified, it should be identified at this time using reference materials.

Example for filling in the field data form:

Field Data Form – Variable Circular Plot Counts (Form 1)

LocationID: _TAPRTweety103_   or Park: _TAPR_   and Location Description: _____

Survey: _May 2001_   Date (mm/dd/yyyy): _05/23/2001_   Start Time (hhmm): _0916_   Observer Initials: _DGP_

Conditions:
Temperature (C): _8.0_   Wind (0-6): _1_   Rain (0-5): _0_   Clouds (0-100): _30_   Noise (0-3): _0_   Protocol Version: _1.0 May 2002_

Time Interval	Observ. #	Species	Distance (m)	DT	Sex	Age	Flock Size	Prev. Plot	# Fly Over	Comments
0-3	1	WEME	35	4	M	A	1			
0-3	2	BHCO	56	4	M	A	1			
0-3	3	HOLA	30	4	M	A	1			
0-3	4	CLSW							1	
3-5	5	GRSP	22	2	M	A	1			

In the example above, four birds were detected during the first 3 minutes of the count, and one (the Grasshopper Sparrow GRSP) was detected during the second 2 minutes of the count. The first record, a Western Meadowlark (WEME) was heard, and then when the observer searched for it, it was seen at a distance of 35 m. The observer therefore recorded the DT Detection Type of 4 since it was heard and then seen. The bird was a male adult. The same occurred for the next two detections: a Brown-headed Cowbird (BHCO) was heard and then seen at a distance of 56 m, and a Horned Lark (HOLA) was heard and then seen at a distance of 30 m. When the Horned Lark was first seen it was flying at a distance of 30 m from the observer, and then landed about 80 m away. The distance of 30 m was recorded since that was the distance at which it was first detected. Also during the first 3 minutes of the count, a Cliff Swallow (CLSW) flew high across the plot and out of view. It was recorded as a flyover. No distance, sex or age was recorded for the flyover. Finally, about 4 minutes into the count, the observer spotted a Grasshopper Sparrow foraging in the grass about 22 m away. After it was spotted, it gave a call, but the DT was recorded as a 2 since it was seen before it was heard.

43

Field Data Form – Variable Circular Plot Counts (Form 1)

LocationID: _____ or Park: _____ and Location Description: _____

Survey: _____ Date (mm/dd/yyyy): _____ Start Time (hhmm): _____ Observer Initials: _____

Conditions:
Temperature (C): _____ Wind (0-6): _____ Rain (0-5): _____ Clouds (0-100): _____ Noise (0-3): _____ Protocol Version: _____

Time Interval	Observ. #	Species	Distance (m)	DT	Sex	Age	Flock Size	Prev. Plot	# Fly Over	Comments
0-3	1									

44

Variable Circular Plot Count Data Form: Categories, Definitions and Descriptions.

Codes (Beaufort scale) used to record wind strength during bird counts.

Wind Code	Explanation
0	Calm, smoke rises vertically (< 2 km/h)
1	Smoke drifts (2-5 km/h)
2	Light breeze felt on face, leaves rustle (6-12 km/h)
3	Leaves and twigs in constant motion (13-19 km/h)
4	Small branches move, raises loose paper, dust rises (20-29 km/h)
5	Fresh breeze, small trees sway (30-39 km/h)
6	Strong breeze, large branches moving, wind whistling (40-50 km/h)

Codes used to record precipitation during bird counts.

Rain Code	Explanation
0	No rain
1	Mist or fog
2	Light drizzle
3	Light rain
4	Heavy rain; difficult to hear birds
5	Snow

Codes used to record level of background noise as it effects observer's ability to hear birds.

Noise Code	Explanation
0	quiet; normal background noises; no interference
1	low noise; might be missing some high-pitched songs/calls of distant birds
2	medium noise; detection radius is probably substantially reduced
3	high noise; probably detecting only the loudest/closest birds

Codes used to record the type of detection (Detection Type, DT) of birds during a count.

DT Code	Explanation
1	heard first, but not seen (i.e., detected initially by sound) during the 5-minute count
2	seen first (regardless of whether it was later heard or not) during the 5-minute count
4	heard first, but then seen (a DT of 1 can be changed to a 4) during the 5-minute count
8	heard between plots or not within the 5-minute sampling period
9	seen between plots or not within the 5-minute sampling period

Breeding Bird Monitoring Protocol for the Heartland Network Inventory and Monitoring Program

Standard Operation Procedure 6: Documenting Habitat Variables

Version 2.00 (05/09/2008)

Revision History Log:

Previous Version #	Revision Date	Author	Changes Made	Reason for Change	New Version #
1.00	May 2008	D.G. Peitz	Entire document	Edited to reflect changes in horizontal profile measures and subplots sampled	2.00

This SOP gives step-by-step instructions for measuring bird habitat composition and structure at park units within the Heartland Network Inventory and Monitoring Program (HTLN). This SOP describes the procedure for establishing the 50.0-m habitat plot, and 1.78- and 5-m sampling subplots. This SOP also describes the procedure for collecting data and filling in the "Field Data Form - Bird Habitat Monitoring Data Sheet" (Form 2).

I. Procedure

1. The sequence in which plots are sampled for habitat measurements follows the order plots are selected for VCP bird counts that day. To avoid biasing bird counts, habitat sampling should begin on a plot after the bird surveyor has completed the count and moved to the next plot, or take place after bird surveys have ceased for the day. Changing habitat conditions due to plant growth and/or grazing requires habitat sampling to be completed by June 30.

2. Sampling will start as soon as the first bird plot for that day has been completed. Observers should stay back from the plot until the count is complete to avoid disturbing the birds. Two-way radios work well to communicate when a plot is ready for habitat sampling. It takes approximately 10 minutes to complete habitat sampling for each VCP point. A minimum of two people are required for the habitat work, with the birder joining them after that day's survey is done.

3. Habitat measurements are taken for a large (50-m radius) plot centered on the bird survey point, as well as permanent subplots within each plot (Figure 6.1).

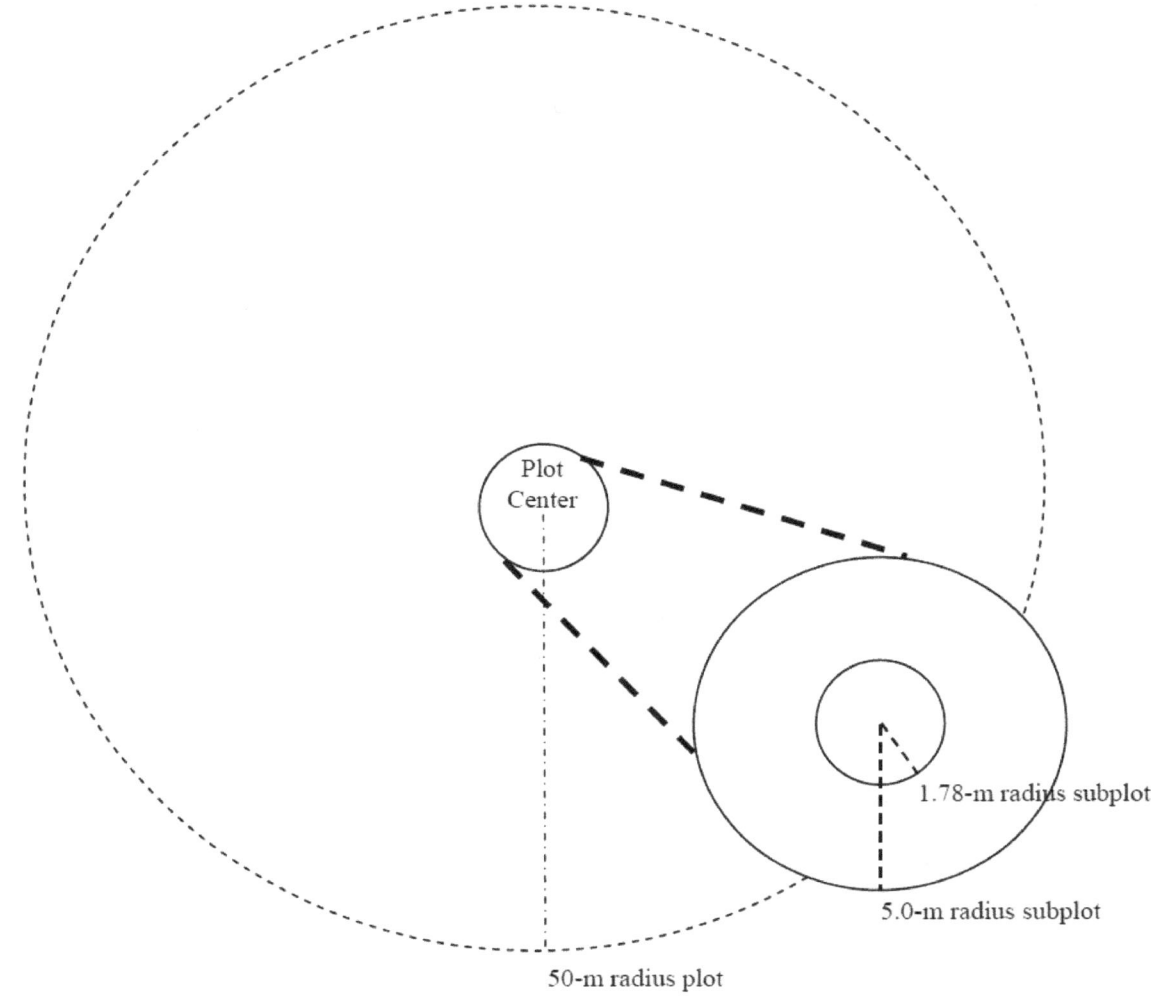

Plot
Center

1.78-m radius subplot

5.0-m radius subplot

50-m radius plot

Figure 6.1. Layout of a 50.0-m radius bird habitat plot and associated 1.78- and 5-m habitat sampling subplots.

4. Two nested circular sampling plots, one 10 m^2 and the other 78.5 m^2 in area, anchored to the center of each subplot with a surveyor's pin make up the permanent subplots (Figure 6.1). A rope the length of each sampling plot radius (1.78-m and 5.0-m, respectively) is run from plot center to the perimeter. Surveyor pins work well to delineate the perimeter of the 10-m^2 sampling plot. Ground cover and vegetation foliar cover are recorded within the smaller sample subplot; tree density and vegetation profile are measured on the larger sample subplot.

5. Navigate to the coordinates of the next plot on the list using the GPS unit (if available) or a compass. The bird surveyor will have marked all completed plots with 36-in pin flags for easy visibility by the habitat crew. The pin flag will be picked up once habitat measures are taken on a plot.

6. Use a new copy of the "Bird Habitat Monitoring Data Sheet" (Form 2) for each habitat plot. Record the following information on each habitat data sheet:

Park Code: A four letter alpha code unique to a particular park (i.e. "ARPO" for Arkansas Post National Memorial, Arkansas; "TAPR" for Tallgrass Prairie National Preserve, Kansas; etc).

Date: The month (mm) / day (dd) / year (yy) data is collected.

Observer Initials: The initials of the first, middle, and last name of each person in the field crew collecting data.

Management Unit: Pasture name or park sub-unit where the variable circular plot is found (i.e. Windmill, Gashouse, etc.); this can be left blank for parks with no named sub-units.

Plot: The permanent identification number assigned to a variable circular plot.

Riparian Corridor: Circle "Yes" or "No" depending on whether or not the plot being sampled is one specifically located in a riparian stratum.

50-m Radius Plot Attributes

Slope: Slope of the ground across the entire 50-m radius plot is measured using an English clinometer. For slope measurements, use two poles of equal length (1 m) to sight between, and read slope directly off the left-hand scale (degrees slope) of the clinometer (Figure 6.2). The poles should be positioned at a distance great enough to capture the average slope of the land across the 50-m radius plot. Slope is measured in degrees the first time a plot is measured and is not recorded in subsequent years.
　　Var: Circle high, medium or low to describe the up and down variability in the slope across the entire 50-m radius plot.

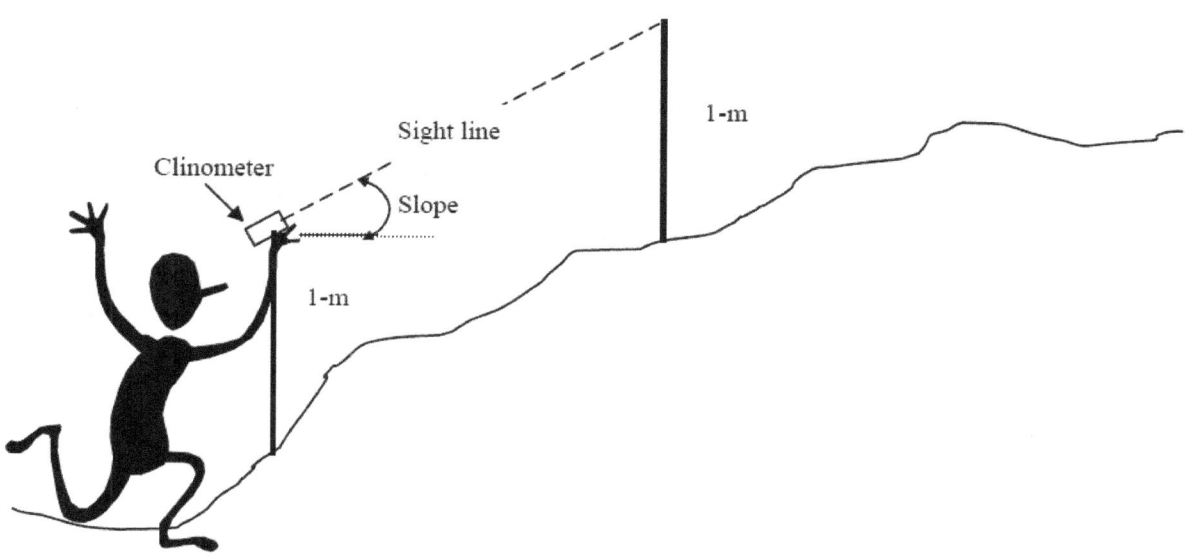

Figure 6.2. A diagram of measuring slope using a clinometer and sighting poles.

<u>Aspect</u>: The slope direction of the 50-m radius plot. Compass readings will be taken with the declination set at 0°. Aspect is recorded from 0° to 359°, with 360° recorded as 0°. Aspect is measured when the plot is established and is not recorded in subsequent years.

    <u>Var</u>: Circle high, medium or low to describe the variability in the direction of the slope across the entire 50-m radius plot.

<u>Topographic Position</u>: Circle the most descriptive word for the location of the 50-m radius plot relative to its local position on the earth's surface.

- Level – level top of a plateau or valley floor or shoreline representing the former position of an alluvial plain, lake or shore.
- Lower-slope – inner gently inclined surface at the base of a slope, generally concave in surface profile. This includes toe slope, the outermost gently inclined surface at the base of a slope, commonly gentle and linear in surface profile.
- Mid-slope – (transportational midslope) – intermediate slope position.
- Upper-slope (shoulder slope) – the uppermost inclined surface at the top of a slope, typically convex in profile.
- Escarpment/face – sloping or vertical side of a stream bank or former stream bank.
- Ledge (terrace, step in slope) – nearly level shelf interrupting a steep slope or cliff face.
- Crest (interfluve, summit, ridge) – linear top of a ridge, hill or mountain; the elevated area between two drainageways that sheds water to the drainageway.
- Depression – bowl shaped or similarly depressed area.
- Draw – depressed V-shaped drainage that carries water toward a stream.

Vegetation Type: An ocular estimate of the percent coverage of habitat types (Table 6.1.) on the 50-m radius plot. Cover is estimated within modified Daubenmire (1959) cover classes, following standard HTLN procedures (Table 6.2).

Table 6.1. Habitat types on 50-m radius plots (includes non-vegetation railroad track habitat type)

Habitat type	Habitat type	Habitat type
Brome Field	Lawn	Shrub
Corn Field	Old Field	Soybean Field
Disturbed Floodplain	Open Woodland	Trail
Disturbed Prairie	Parking Lot	Tree Line
Drainage	Railroad Tracks	Upland prairie
Fescue/Orchard Grass	Restored Prairie	Western Wheatgrass
Field/Prairie	Riparian Prairie	Wetland
Floodplain	Riparian Woodland	Woodland
Highway Right of Way	River Terraces	Woodland Swamp
Intermittent Water Cover	Seep	Other

Table 6.2. Cover is estimated within modified Daubenmire (1959) cover classes.

Cover class	Explanation
0	None present
1	0 – 1 % coverage of measured variable
2	1 – 5 % coverage of measured variable
3	5 – 25 % coverage of measured variable
4	25 – 50 % coverage of measured variable
5	50 – 75 % coverage of measured variable
6	75 – 95 % coverage of measured variable
7	95 – 100 % coverage of measured variable

Road Cover: An ocular estimate of the percent of ground covered by pasture or paved roadway on the 50-m radius plot. Estimates of cover will be in standard HTLN cover classes for both paved and pasture roads (Table 6.2).

Water Cover: An ocular estimate of the percent of ground covered by pond or stream on the 50-m radius plot. Estimates of cover will be in standard HTLN cover classes for both streams and ponds (Table 6.2).

Plot Notes: This space is provided to record comments on the 50-m radius plot.

5-m Radius Subplot Attributes

Slope: Slope of the ground across the subplot is measured using an English clinometer. Slope is measured in degrees with a clinometer the first time a subplot is measured and is not recorded in subsequent years. For slope measurements, use two poles of equal length (1 m) to sight between and read slope directly off the left-hand scale (slope) of the clinometer (Figure 6.2). The poles should be positioned at a distance great enough to capture the average slope of the land across the subplot.

Aspect: The slope direction of the subplot. Compass readings will be taken with the declination set at $0°$. Aspect is recorded from $0°$ to $359°$, with $360°$ recorded as $0°$. Aspect is measured when the plot is established and is not recorded in subsequent years.

Tree Tally: Tree species are recorded using a code consisting of the first three letters of the individual's genus name, followed by a space and then the first three letters of the species epithet. Counts are taken on all tree species within the 5.0-m radius subplot. Trees greater than 1.5 m in height will be dot tallied (Table 6.3) by species in size classes based on diameter at breast height (i.e. 1.5 m above ground).

- less than 1.0-cm in diameter
- 1.1-2.5 cm diameter
- 2.6-8.0 cm diameter
- 8.1-15.0 cm diameter
- 15.1-23.0 cm diameter
- 23.1-38.0 cm diameter
- greater than 38.0 cm diameter

Table 6.3. Dot tallies are recorded as follow and repeated for the next count of ten trees and so on.

One tree	Two trees	Three trees	Four trees	Five trees
•	• •	• • •	• • • •	•—• • •
Six trees	Seven trees	Eight trees	Nine Trees	Ten trees
⌐	⊓	□	⊠	⊠

Canopy Height: Canopy heights of hardwood and coniferous trees are measured to a 1/4 meter with a metric clinometer equipped with 15-m and 20-m scales (Figure 6.3). When measured from a distance of 15 m or 20 m, tree heights can be read directly from the instrument's scales. The readings should be doubled when measuring from distances of 30 m or 40 m. The actual measurement of a tree's height is done by an observer sighting the top of the tree with both eyes open and reading the numeric value on the scale (right scale for 15 m and left scale for 20 m distance) where the hair line crosses. This gives a height of a tree (canopy) from eye level. The observer then measures from eye level to the base of the tree at ground level. Canopy height is the height of the tree +/- the height of the tree from eye level to the ground. If the base of the tree is above eye level the value read is positive and will need to be subtracted from the height of the tree from eye level to the top of the tree. If the base of the tree is below eye level the value read is negative and it will need to be added to the height of the tree from eye level to the top of the tree. Total canopy height is the height of the tallest tree recorded, hardwood or coniferous.

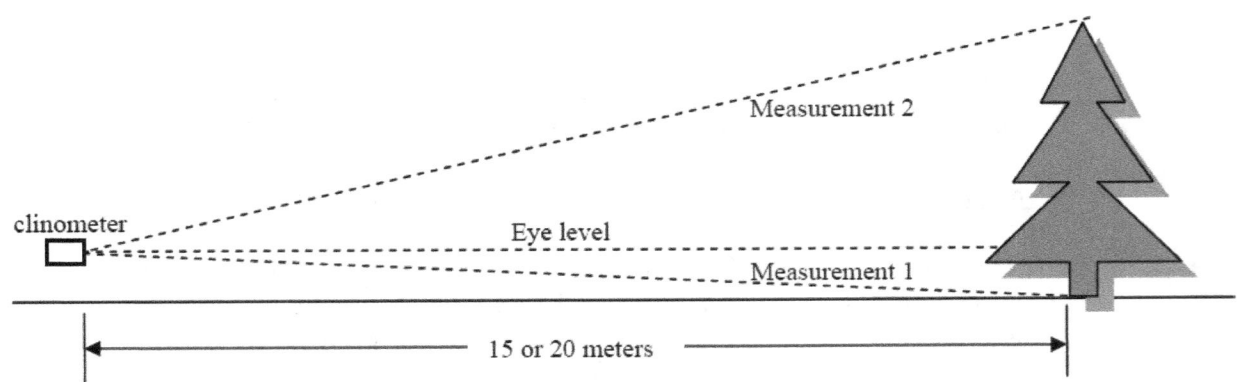

Figure 6.3. Using a clinometer to measure tree height. Tree height is taken at a distance of 15 (right scale) or 20 m (left scale) depending on the height of the tree. Trees greater than 20 m should be measured at a distance of 30 (right scale) or 40 m (left scale) and the clinometer reading doubled. Measurement 1 should be added to measurement 2 if it is a negative number and subtracted if it is positive to obtain tree height.

Canopy Cover: The spherical densiometer consists of a concave mirror with 24, 1/4 inch squares engraved on the surface (Figure 6.4). Take four densiometer readings from the center of each subplot, one in each of the cardinal directions. Hold the instrument level over the center stake, and 12" to 18" in front of body, at breast height, so that operator's head is just outside of the grid area. Assume four equally-spaced dots in each square of the grid and systematically count dots equivalent to quarter-square canopy cover. Remember that there are a total of 96 quarter-squares represented on the mirror. That is, if you count canopy openings rather than canopy closure, subtract from 96 to obtain canopy coverage. The number of dots covered by canopy will be converted to percent canopy coverage (multiplied by 1.04) during the data summary process. Record hardwood, conifer, and total canopy cover separately.

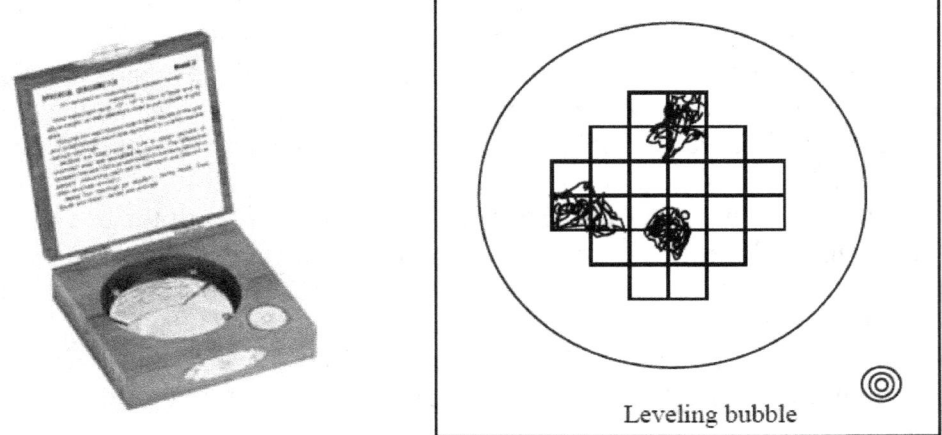

Figure 6.4. Spherical densiometer showing a dot count of 20 (photograph courtesy of Forestry Suppliers.

<u>Basal Area</u>: Basal area of hardwood and conifer species is estimated using a 10-factor English cruz-all (Figure 6.5). Holding the button at the end of the chain in your teeth (or against your chin), extend the cruz-all angle gauge away from your eye until the chain is taut. Keeping your eye directly over the subplot center, look through the cruz-all at every tree around you. Count trees that appear as wide or wider, at breast height, than the opening for the basal area factor you are using (10). Tree counts will be converted to basal area estimates (m^2/ha) during the data summary process by multiplying counts by 2.5. Count hardwood and conifer species separately. Total basal area is the combined basal area of hardwood and pines.

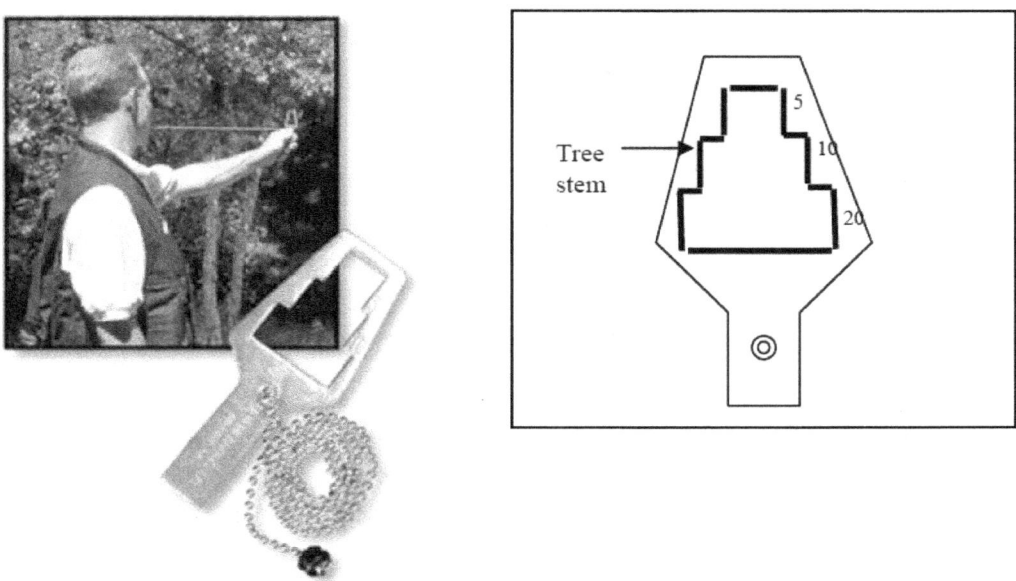

Figure 6.5. Using a cruz-all to count trees for basal area estimates. Count trees with the 10 factor opening on the cruz-all.

<u>Horizontal Vegetation Profile</u>: Vegetation profile readings are taken by an observer located a distance of 15 m perpendicular to the profile board (located at plot center) at an azimuth direction of 0° (compass declination is set at 0°). The observer utilizes a pole marked at 0.5, 1.0, and 1.5 m above the ground to adjust their eye position as they read the board from bottom to top (Figure 6.6). Stratum 0-0.25 and 0.25-0.50 should be read from 0.5 m, stratum 0.50-0.75, 0.75-1.0, and 1.0-1.25 should be read from 1.0 m and remaining strata should be read from a height of 1.5 m. Observers should site with one eye to prevent parallax problems. The area of the profile board obscured by vegetation, both live and standing dead, between the board and observer is measured using a modified Daubenmire cover class value (Table 6.2) for each of the strata marked on the board.

Observer height intervals:

Stratum	Observer height
0.00-0.25	0.5
0.25-0.50	0.5
0.50-0.75	1.0
0.75-1.00	1.0
1.00-1.25	1.0
1.25-1.50	1.5
1.50-1.75	1.5
1.75-2.00	1.5

Figure 6.6. Conducting the horizontal cover measurements using profile board and sighting pole.

Vertical Profile of Vegetation: Vertical vegetation profile is measured using a 7.5-m rod marked in meter intervals. Touches or 'hits' of vegetation against the rod are recorded in each interval for deciduous "D", herbaceous "H" and/or coniferous "C" vegetation. Measurements are taken on the periphery of a 5-m radius subplot in the four cardinal directions, north, south, east and west; therefore, the maximum number of 'hits' per increment for each vegetation type is four. See Figure 6.7 for an example of how to measure the vertical profile of vegetation.

Figure 6.7. Conducting the vertical profile measurements using a 7.5-m measuring rod. As shown in the figure to the right, a conifer touches the measuring rod between 0 – 1, 1 – 2, 2 -3 and 3 – 4 m increments. Herbaceous vegetation touches the measuring rod between 0 and 1 m.

1.78-m Radius Subplot Attributes

Ground Cover: An ocular estimate of ground cover is made within a 10-m² (1.78-m radius) sampling plot centered on each subplot. Cover of the ground surface is estimated within modified Daubenmire cover classes (Table 6.2). Percent ground cover is estimated for the following parameters:
- Deciduous Leaf Litter: deciduous woody leaf litter.
- Conifer Litter: conifer leaf litter and organic debris.
- Grass Litter: grass and grass-like plant litter.
- Bare Soil: soil surface not covered by litter, plant or rock.
- Bare Rock: visible rocks in the plot.
- Woody Debris: ground covered by woody debris including twigs and stems.
- Unvegetated: 100 – total basal cover of the vegetation (percent).

Foliar Cover: An ocular estimate of foliar cover is made within a 10-m² (1.78-m radius) sampling plot centered on each subplot. The estimate is a vertical projection of foliar cover onto the ground surface. Cover is estimated within modified Daubenmire cover classes (Table 6.2). If a cover category is not present in the plot, enter a 0 for that parameter – do not leave empty records. Percent foliar cover is estimated for the following plant guilds:
- Warm-season grasses; warm season grasses.
- Cool-season grasses; includes graminoid species (e.g. sedges).

- Forbs; includes yucca, cactus, ferns and other herbaceous vascular plants.
- Moss and lichen; mosses and lichens.
- Woody shrubs and vines; woody shrubs and vines rooted in the plot.
- Tree Seedlings; includes seedlings less than 1.5 m in height.
- Total Foliar Cover; vertical projection of total foliar cover of living vegetation (less than 1.5 m in height) onto the ground surface.

See HTLN vegetation monitoring database for park specific plant species included in each foliar coverage guild.

Field Data Form - Bird Habitat Monitoring Data Sheet (Form 2)
Park Code: _____ **Date** (mm/dd/yyyy) _____ **Observer(s) Initials:** _____

Management Unit: _____ **Plot:** _____ **Riparian Corridor:** Yes No

PLOT ATTRIBUTES: (50-m radius)

Slope ($^\circ$): _____ **Var:** high med low **Aspect** ($^\circ$): _____ **Var:** high med low

Topographic position:
level   lower-slope   mid-slope   upper-slope   escarpment/face   ledge   crest   depression   draw

Vegetation Type:	Cover Class:	Vegetation Type:	Cover Class:	Road Cover:	Cover Class:
				Paved	
				Pasture	
			Water	Cover:	
				Stream	
				Pond	

Plot Notes: _____

SUBPLOT: _____ **Random Azimuth** ($^\circ$) _____ **Slope**($^\circ$): _____ **Aspect** ($^\circ$) _____

TREE TALLY (by dbh size class)

Species	<1.0 cm	1.1 – 2.5 cm	2.6 – 8.0 cm	8.1 – 15.0 cm	15.1 – 23.0 cm	23.1 – 38.0 cm	>38.0 cm

CANOPY HEIGHT: (m)   **CANOPY COVER**: (dots covered out of 96)   **BASAL AREA**:
Hardwood: _____   Hardwood: 1 ___ 2 ___ 3 ___ 4 ___   Hardwood: _____
Conifer: _____   Conifer: 1 ___ 2 ___ 3 ___ 4 ___   Conifer: _____
   Total: 1 ___ 2 ___ 3 ___ 4 ___

GROUND COVER:	Cover Class:	FOLIAR COVER (by guilds):	Cover Class:
Deciduous Leaf Litter		Warm Season Grass	
Conifer Leaf Litter		Cool Season Grass	
Grass Litter		Forbs	
Bare Soil		Moss and Lichen	
Rock		Shrubs & Vines	
Woody Debris		Tree Seedlings	
Unvegetated		Total Foliar Cover (< 1.5 m tall)	

HORIZONTAL VEGETATION PROFILE BOARD: (measured at a distance of 15-m true North)

0.25 m: _____   0.50 m: _____   0.75 m: _____   1.0 m: _____   1.25 m: _____   1.5 m: _____   1.75 m: _____   2.0 m: _____

VEGETATION PROFILE (D = Deciduous, H = Herbaceous, C = Conifer)

0–1 m	1–2 m	2–3 m	3–4 m	4–5 m	5–6 m	6–7 m	7–7.5 m

Prairie Bird Habitat Data Form: Categories, Definitions and Descriptions.

50-m VEGETATION TYPE (includes non-vegetation habitat types)

Brome Field	Lawn	Shrub
Corn Field	Old Field	Soybean Field
Disturbed Floodplain	Open Woodland	Trail
Disturbed Prairie	Parking Lot	Tree Line
Drainage	Railroad Tracks	Upland prairie
Fescue/Orchard Grass	Restored Prairie	Western Wheatgrass
Field/Prairie	Riparian Prairie	Wetland
Floodplain	Riparian Woodland	Woodland
Highway Right of Way	River Terraces	Woodland Swamp
Intermittent Water Cover	Seep	Other

COVER CLASS DEFINITIONS AND CUTPOINT DESCRIPTIONS

Cover class	Definition	Upper cutpoints for 50-m radius plot	Upper cutpoints for 5-m radius plot	Upper cutpoints for 1.78-m radius plot
0	None present			
1	Trace to 1 %	A circle of radius 5.00 m	A circle of radius 0.50 m	A circle of radius 0.18 m
2	1 – 5 %	A circle of radius 11.18 m	A circle of radius 1.12 m	A circle of radius 0.40 m
3	5 – 25 %	A circle of radius 25.00 m	A circle of radius 2.50 m	A circle of radius 0.89 m
4	25 – 50 %	A circle of radius 35.36-m	A circle of radius 3.54-m	A circle of radius 1.26-m
5	50 – 75 %	A circle of radius 43.30 m	A circle of radius 4.33 m	A circle of radius 1.54 m
6	75 – 95 %	A circle of radius 48.73 m	A circle of radius 4.87 m	A circle of radius 1.73 m
7	95 – 100 %	Full plot radius	Full plot radius	Full plot radius

HORIZONTAL VEGETATION PROFILE BOARD INCREMENTS and OBSERVATION HEIGHTS

Stratum	Observer height
0.00-0.25	0.5
0.25-0.50	0.5
0.50-0.75	1.0
0.75-1.00	1.0
1.00-1.25	1.0
1.25-1.50	1.5
1.50-1.75	1.5
1.75-2.00	1.5

Breeding Bird Monitoring Protocol for the Heartland Network Inventory and Monitoring Program

Standard Operation Procedure 7: Data Management

Version 2.00 (05/09/2008)

Revision History Log:

Previous Version #	Revision Date	Author	Changes Made	Reason for Change	New Version #

This SOP describes procedures for managing the Heartland Network Inventory and Monitoring Program (HTLN) database for bird communities. Specifically, this document addresses procedures for data entry, verification, validation, export to outside systems, security and availability. Parks are referenced throughout the database using the standard National Park Service four-letter abbreviations. Database users should become familiar with the park abbreviations. Park names, abbreviations and links to internet URLs are available through the opening form (the "Switchboard") of the database.

Database design is critical to understanding how to use a database effectively. This SOP describes database design issues that have been addressed by the NPS Inventory and Monitoring (I&M) Program (National Park Service 2006) and database design issues specific to the HTLN bird database.

Data management can be divided into (a) the initial design phase that involves defining the data model, its entities and their relationships and (b) the procedures necessary to implement the database. Microsoft (MS) Access 2003 is the primary software used for maintaining bird community data. Environmental Systems Research Institute (ESRI) ArcInfo 9.x is used for managing spatial data associated with field sampling locations. Data products derived from this project will be available at the NPS I&M Data Store and directly from the Heartland Network. QA/QC guidelines in this document are based on recommendations of Rowell et al. (2005) and citations therein.

I. Data Model

The database is named 'Tweety'. It has a hierarchical design based on Natural Resource Database Template (NRDT) (National Park Service 2006). Locations and sampling periods are maintained at the top (they relate one-to-many with other tables in the database).

Tweety contains 23 data tables (including look-up, enumeration and reference tables). To simplify data management, Tweety can be viewed as two sets of tables linked by Location and Sampling Period. One set stores bird observations and associated weather conditions while the other stores information about the habitat. Sampling periods (temporal resolution = the duration of the field trip to a specific Park unit), sampling events (temporal resolution = nearest minute during observations) and sampling locations form the core tables. The core tables capture the field sample occasion (the when and where of the sample).

Bird monitoring data are stored in tables that link to these core tables. An entity relationship diagram of the basic design is given in Figure 7.1.

The figure depicts information such as date and time, location and park/project codes. It also includes bird monitoring data and examples of habitat data (vegetation type and ground cover type) collected in association with bird observations. Other tables (not shown here) include weather data and other habitat factors such as horizontal and vertical vegetative structure, tree counts, tree basal area, canopy cover, canopy height and foliar cover type. The diagram shows the temporal resolution for bird observations to be to the nearest minute while habitat data are collected to the nearest sampling period (a field trip lasting several days). Differences in sampling design are explained in SOP's #9.5 "Conducting the Variable Circular Plot Count" and SOP #9.6 "Documenting Habitat Variables".

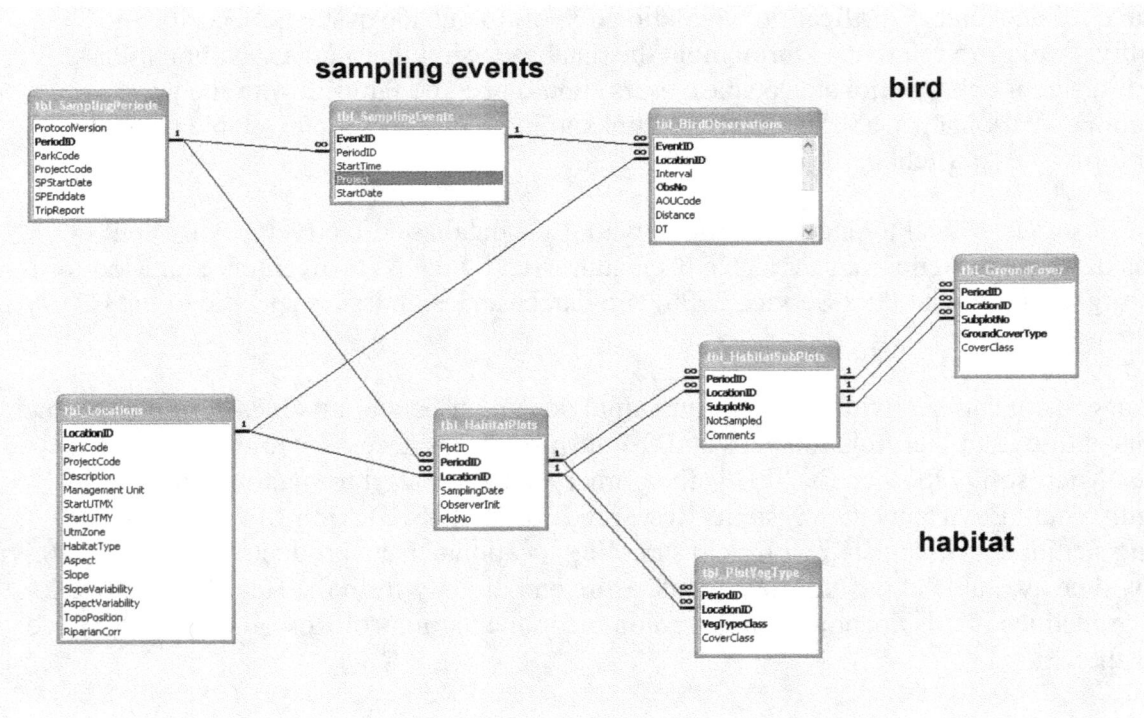

Figure 7.1. Data model for Tweety 7.0. Bird data are collected and managed at a much higher temporal resolution than habitat data.

II. Data Preparation

Quality assurance and quality control procedures related to data recording are important components of any project. Sampling data (i.e., sample methods, effort, weather/water quality conditions, and species abundance data) are recorded and checked for completeness either before leaving a site or within 24 hours of data recording. This will aid in verification and validation of the data after entry into the database. To prevent the complete loss of field form data due to unforeseen circumstances (i.e., fire or flood in the workplace), all field sheets are photocopied and a hard copy is stored in a separate location than the original. Field sheets are scanned into a computer and electronic copies of the data sheets stored on the HTLN server located at Wilson's Creek National Battlefield, Republic, MO. This will ensure that at least one copy of the field sheets is available for data entry and verification.

III. Data Entry

Data entry is accomplished using Access forms and tables. Upon opening the database, the switchboard appears (Figure 7.2). Navigate to each data-entry form using the switchboard. An overview of the major data-entry forms is given in Figure 7.3.

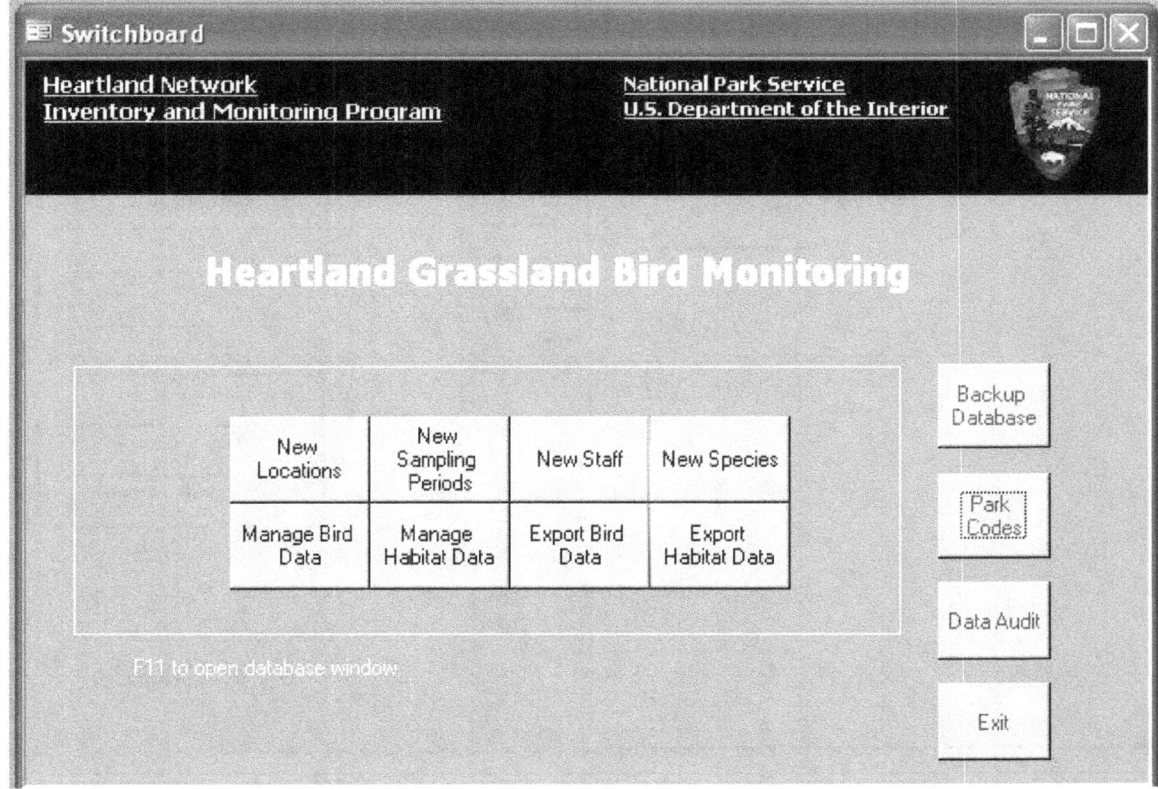

Figure 7.2. Tweety database switchboard.

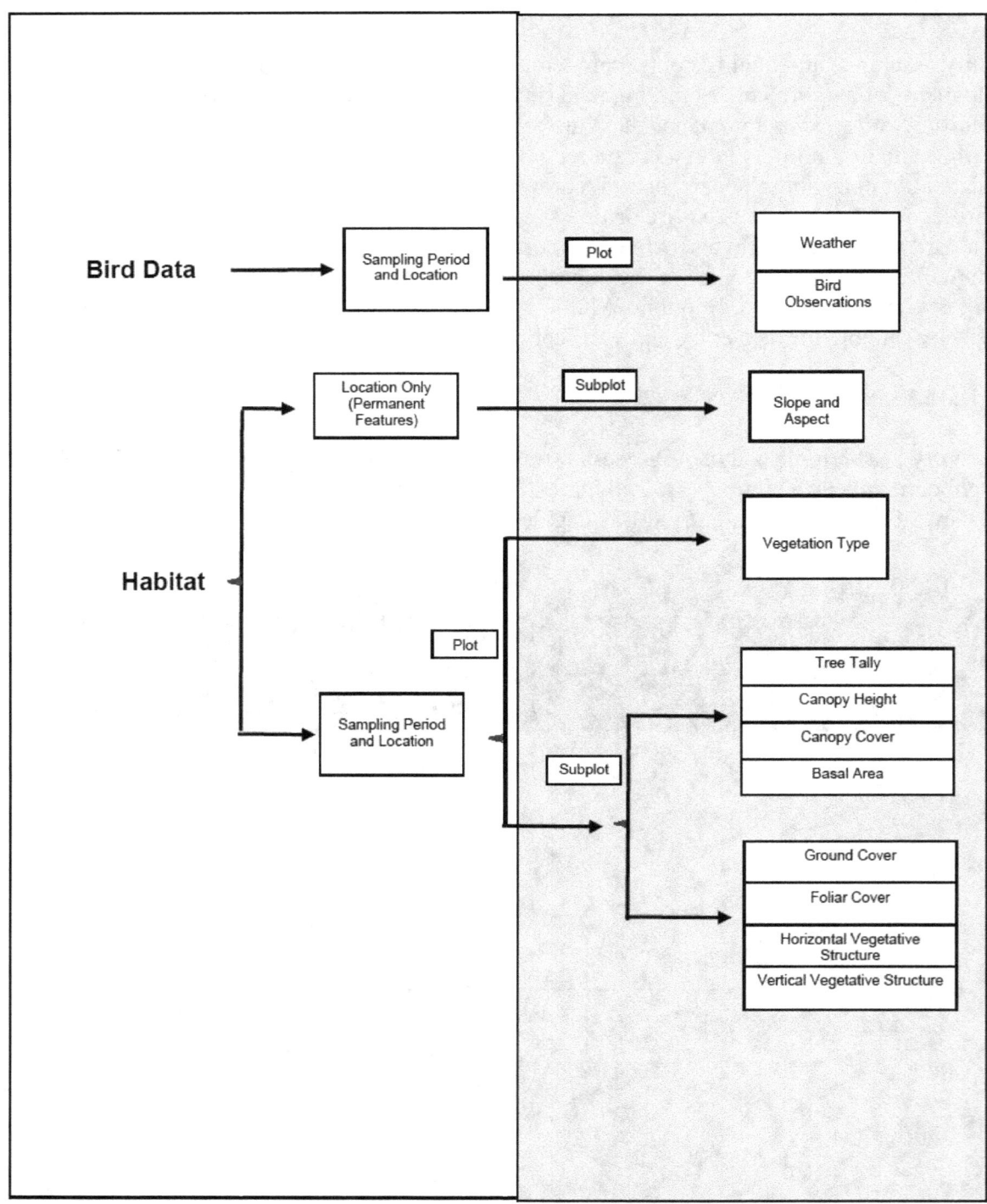

Figure 7.3. Outline of bird monitoring data-entry forms. Note: Forms are selected from the main switchboard (bird or habitat data buttons) and data are entered into subforms (shaded area).

Bird Data Entry

Bird data entry is a derived process from the legacy Tweety database (Peitz et al. 2003). EventIDs are used to increase temporal specificity of PeriodID. Location and time information are stored in key fields LocationID, PeriodID and EventID (see Table 7.1). A key is a column in a table dedicated to linking to other tables. In other words, keys are the fields that create the relationships between tables.

Table 7.1. Three key fields used in the Tweety database are shown.

Table Name	Key Field	Example (record value)
tbl_Location	LocationID	LIBOTweety41
tbl_SamplingPeriod	PeriodID	LIBOTweety2007Jun09
tbl_SamplingEvent	EventID	LIBOTweety2007Jun100715

Staff should add new records to tbl_Location only when new sampling sites are established at a park. Data-entry forms will automatically generate EventID values. The main area of concern is the tbl_SamplingPeriod table. Staff should ensure that the necessary PeriodID record is included in the tbl_SamplingPeriod table prior to data entry. After updates to sampling data (LocationID and PeriodID), the user can begin to enter bird and habitat monitoring data.

Entering Sampling Occasion Data

Procedures:

1. Open the database. Click on the Backup Database button to the left. This will save a copy of the database including today's date in the filename. Store your backups in some standard location that will be copied to tape or other standard backups periodically. If you run into trouble, you can fall back on this copy.

2. Reopen the database. Click on the New Locations button. Verify that all of the locations that you will need for data entry are included on this table. If you have new locations, insert them on the bottom of the table. They will be sorted alphabetically when the table is reopened. Close the table by clicking the red X on the upper right.

3. Click on the New Sampling Periods. Verify that there is an entry for the year and park for the data you wish to enter. Make a new entry if required. Close the table by clicking the red X on the upper right of the table.

4. Click on the "Manage Bird Data" button. This will open the main window for managing bird data (see Figure 7.4).

5. Choose "Enter New Data". Enter LocationID and PeriodID from the combo boxes.

6. Enter the field date and time. EventID will be generated when you tab from the "Time" entry field.

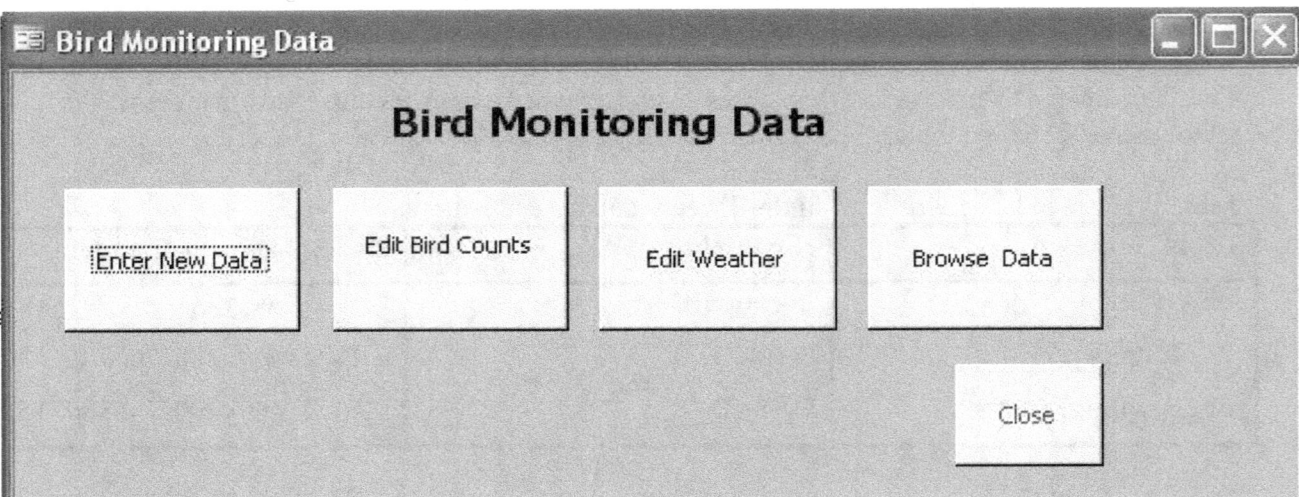

Figure 7.4. Main window for entering bird data.

Entering Weather Data

Procedures:

1. Click on the Sampling Event Conditions button.

2. Enter temperature, rain, clouds, noise and any comments. Data-entry checks limit the range of values for the first four fields.

Entering Bird Observations

Procedures:

1. From the Sampling Event Conditions window, click on the 'Enter Bird Observations' button.

2. From the field data sheet, enter the time interval, observation number, bird species, distance (if known), detection type (DT), sex, age, flocksize, whether or not the bird was a 'flyover'.

3. Click on the 'continue' button to add additional observed species to this event (total duration = five minutes) or click on close if there are no further observations.

Habitat Data Entry

Plot and subplot-level data describe the habitat for bird communities for up to four subplots per plot. Permanent features (slope, aspect) are maintained at the subplot level but are only entered once during the lifetime of the sampling location. Other factors vary by season. Vegetation Type at the plot level is maintained by Location ID and PeriodID. Procedures for data-entry for this table are after the subplot features form. LocationID, PeriodID and Subplot number are the key fields that maintain subplot habitat relationships. Subplot values are entered along with field data. In addition to the permanent subplot features, there are eight sections of subplot data: Tree Tally, Canopy Height, Canopy Cover, Basal Area, Ground Cover, Foliar Cover, Horizontal Vegetative Structure, and Vertical Vegetative Structure.

Entering Permanent Subplot Features

Procedures:

1. From the main switchboard click on "Add Habitat Records"

2. From the intermediate habitat form, select the appropriate LocationID, PeriodID, date and observer initials. Click on "Open Subplot Features Form".

3. Enter each of the permanent feature columns. Currently, LocationID and subplot number must be entered manually. Also enter Random Azimuth, Slope and Aspect. The record will be sorted ascending (LocationID, subplotno) when the table is reopened. Duplicate records for location and subplot are not permitted. Click on the red X on the upper right to close the table.

Entering Habitat Data

Procedures:

1. Click on "Open Habitat Form" from the intermediate habitat form.

2. From the Habitat Plots Form, click on the Vegetation Type button. From the PlotVegType form, choose the different types of vegetation cover and their associated cover classes from the two combo boxes. Click on Continue to add addition records.

3. Click on Return to return to the Habitat Intermediate window.

Entering Subplot Habitat Data

Procedures:

1. From the Habitat Intermediate window, click on "Open Habitat Form".

2. From the Habitat Form, click on the SubPlots button.

3. At this point, you should see the main window for entering subplot habitat data (see Figure 7.5 below).

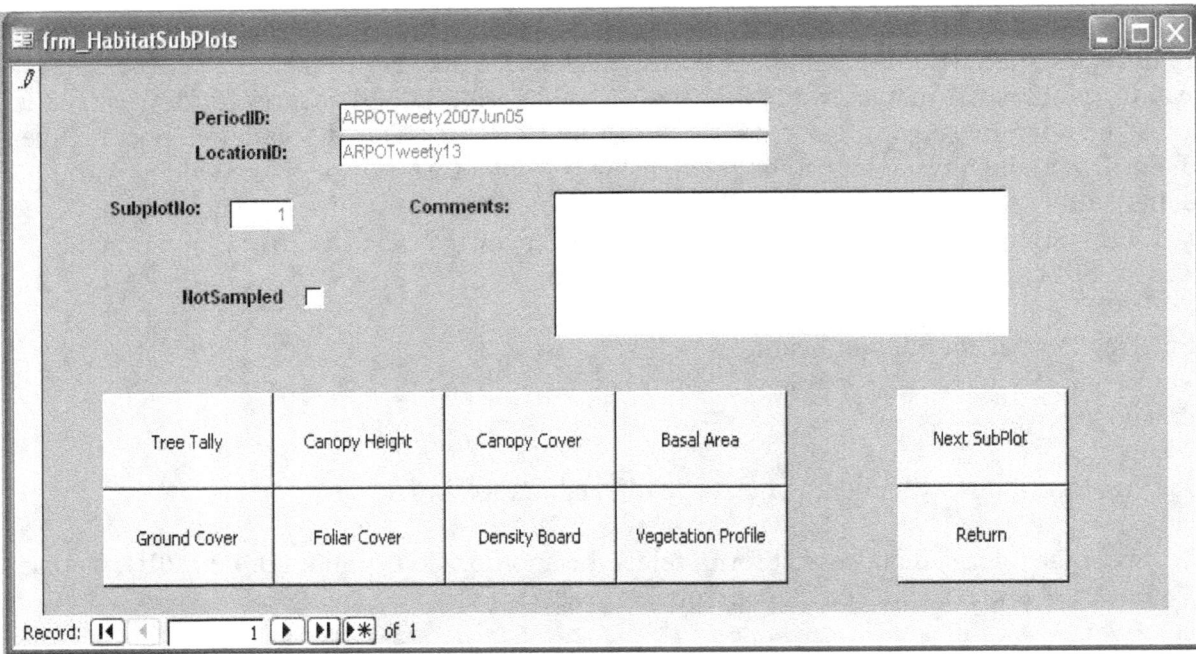

Figure 7.5. Main window for entering subplot habitat data.

4. Subplot data can be entered in any order although the buttons on the top row correspond to the first tables in the field data sheet (woodland characteristics) while the bottom row corresponds to subplot data recorded at all subplot locations.

5. Its best to enter data into each table before proceeding to the next subplot. This will simplify data entry and follow the layout of the field data sheets.

IV. Data Verification

Data verification immediately follows data entry. Computer records are verified for accuracy against paper field data sheets. Hard copy of data records should be used in the verification against field data to minimize proof-reading error. Compare the output directly with original field data sheets to identify missing, mismatched, or redundant records. The verification step should be completed by staff other than those doing data entry if at all possible. Following verification, the project manager should recheck 10% of the records. The verification and recheck steps should be repeated until no errors are discovered

Procedures:

1. Print pertinent data and compare with original field forms

2. Reconcile errors in database

3. Recheck 10% of records. If errors are detected, repeat steps 2 and 3.

V. Data Validation

Data validation involves checking the accuracy of data against outside controls or specifications. Four types of data validation are used with Tweety. They are:

- Referential integrity
- Limited lists for nominal data
- Reasonable values for continuous attribute data
- Reasonable coordinates for spatial data

Referential integrity and data validation for nominal data are typically built into the database and require little or no maintenance. Checking for reasonable values for continuous attribute data and spatial data requires the attention of the project manager and staff familiar with GIS. Knowledge of the sampling design and underlying ecological processes is necessary to identify extreme outliers that are not natural members of the distribution of measured ecological parameters.

Referential Integrity
Referential integrity is a property of the relationships between database tables. You create referential integrity by imposing rules or "constraints" on the relationships between key fields. A key can be either a primary key or a foreign key depending what rules are assigned to it. Primary key values must be unique and cannot be null. Each value in a foreign key must be derived from the domain of its related primary key. Referential constraints prevent dangling references between rows of related tables (Roman, 2002). Furthermore, they reduce the chance of inadvertent record deletions.

Nominal data
Nominal data can be validated during the data-entry process by limiting data-entry to pre-determined values using pick list and combo-box controls on forms. Examples of nominal data in Tweety include LocationID, PeriodID, Species, EventID, ground cover type, foliar cover type and vegetation type. Values should be chosen from lists or combo boxes to the greatest extent possible in the database forms. The forms typically require little or no maintenance.

Continuous data
Validation of continuous data requires the attention of the project manager. Knowledge of the ecological system is necessary to determine what constitutes a reasonable quantitative value for a particular parameter. The data can be exported to a statistical package for quantitative evaluation. Although analysis might be conducted on trimmed distributions, the complete dataset should always be retained to identify possible sources of error.

Procedures:

1. Export the datasets of interest (see Exporting Data, below).

2. Import the data into a spreadsheet or statistical package.

3. Calculate descriptive statistics such as mean, median, standard deviation, range and sample size. Plot a histogram and identify outlier values.

4. Extreme individual values may indicate recording or data-entry errors.

Spatial Data
Spatial validation of sample coordinates can be accomplished using the ArcMap component of ArcGIS. Spatial data are maintained in the project shape file(s) derived from GPS data. They can be added to an ArcMap project and compared with known features on a high resolution orthophoto such as a USGS DOQQ.

Procedures:

1. Develop testing project within ArcMap constrained to appropriate UTM zone and projection (e.g., 15N, NAD83).

2. Add park unit boundaries and any necessary spatial data (roads, water, contour, etc.) for reference.

3. Add relevant site coordinate data to testing project and validate against known features. Use cultural features or significant natural features from a DOQQ or similar product to measure error.

4. Identify errors and determine their cause. Systematic bias may indicate incorrect mapping project settings in the GPS unit. Unusually large error may indicate limited availability of GPS satellites due to tree canopy or other physical structures, GPS operator error or simply orientation issues during field work. Correction of GPS coordinate errors may require site revisits to obtain positional accuracy.

5. Develop metadata for final spatial dataset.

VI. Exporting Data

Monitoring data can be exported from Tweety and imported into software packages such as spreadsheets and statistical packages. Each export category follows the design shown in Figure 7.3. Export data sets are organized by park and year. This organization should facilitate comparison of the same parameters across multiple years and between multiple parameters within years.

Procedures:

1. Click on Export Bird Data from the switchboard.

2. Select year and park code.

3. Click on residency, bird frequency, plot frequency, bird density or bird density of occupied plots for simple initial analyses of bird observation data.

4. To examine habitat data, click on Export Habitat Data from the main switchboard.

5. Each of the habitat tables, as indicated in Figure 7.3 can be exported using a range of years and a given park code.

6. The output is organized by Year, Park, PeriodID and LocationID.

VI. File Organization

The various databases, reports and GIS coverages used and generated by the Heartland Network create a large number of files and folders to manage. Poor file organization can lead to confusion and data corruption. As a standard data management technique, files pertaining to the project are managed in their own folders: Analysis, for data analysis; Data, for copies of archived data as well as data sheets; "Documents", for supporting materials related to the project; and "Spatial info", for GPS and other spatial data. The databases are managed in the "Database" folders and contain prior versions of the database in a "Dev" development subfolder. The use of standardized file-systems is especially critical where multiple parties require access to shared folders, files and data sets. Standardized file-systems are also important to maintain tape back-up systems and to maintain program operations during periods of staff turnover.

VII. Version Control

Prior to any major changes of a data set, a copy is stored with the appropriate version number. This allows for the tracking of changes over time. With proper controls and communication, versioning ensures that only the most current version is used in any analysis. You should consider daily backups using the Access backup feature (which creates a backup file with the date appended to the database name) during periods of active data entry. For archive backups that will be stored permanently, versioning of archived data sets is handled by adding a floating-point number to the file name, with the first version being numbered 1.0. Each major version is assigned a sequentially higher whole number. Each minor version is assigned a sequentially higher .1 number. Major version changes include migrations across Access versions and complete rebuilds of front-ends and analysis tools. Minor version changes include bug fixes in front-end and analysis tools. Frequent users of the data are notified of the updates, and provided with a copy of the most recent archived version.

VIII. Backups

Secure data archiving is essential for protecting data files from corruption. Once a data set has passed the QA/QC procedures specified in the protocol, a new metadata record is created using the NPS Metadata Tools (stand alone or within ArcCatalog) and/or Dataset Catalog. Backup copies of the data are maintained at both on- and off-site locations. An additional digital copy is forwarded to the NPS I&M Data Store. Tape backups and/or hard drive backups of all data are made at regular intervals in accordance with current HTLN backup standard operating procedures and will be made minimally, once per week, with semi-annual tapes permanently archived (refer to Rowell and Williams 2007).

Procedures:

1. Create metadata record pursuant to data archiving.

2. Backup data.

3. Store backup copies on- and off-site and forward a copy to the I&M Data Store.

4. Administer regularly scheduled backups of data.

IX. Data Availability

Currently, data are available for research and management applications for those database versions where all QA/QC has been completed and the data have been archived. Data can be transferred using ftp or by e-mail (where files are smaller than a few megabytes). Monitoring data will become generally available for download directly from the NPS I&M Data Store. Metadata for the bird monitoring database are developed using the NPS Database Metadata Extractor. Metadata will also be available at the NPS I&M Data Store.

Data Manager
Heartland I&M Network
National Park Service
Wilson's Creek National Battlefield
Republic MO 65738

Breeding Bird Monitoring Protocol for the Heartland Network Inventory and Monitoring Program

Standard Operation Procedure 8: Data Analysis

Version 2.00 (05/09/2008)

Revision History Log:

Previous Version #	Revision Date	Author	Changes Made	Reason for Change	New Version #

This SOP gives step-by-step instructions for analyzing variable circular plot (VCP) bird count and habitat survey data collected at parks within the Heartland Network Inventory and Monitoring Program (HTLN). Microsoft Access 2003 is the software environment for data management. This SOP is divided into two sections: Section A; data summary and analysis each time a survey is conducted, and Section B; long-term trend and species-habitat relationship analysis. Each time a survey is conducted, the frequency and abundance of bird species is reported as: (1) individuals/plot visit, (2) proportion of plots occupied, (3) park-wide species density, and (4) localized species densities. Species richness, diversity, and distribution evenness at the plot level should be calculated, and averaged by study unit and/or park-wide. Summaries of habitat attributes at the 5- and 50-m plot level are required for "permanent" and "semi-permanent" features. The bulk of habitat data is collected at the 5-m subplot level. Subplot features that are reported each time a survey is conducted include tree tallies (stems/ha), canopy height, canopy coverage, basal area, ground and foliar coverage, horizontal vegetation coverage and structural diversity. Plot-specific habitat metrics in conjunction with plot specific bird data serve as a first cut in trying to understand habitat use by a species, including species of continental importance. Section B methods consist of: 1) estimating bird species abundance adjusted for detectability (using Distance analysis; this method is included with "long-term" analyses because not all observations are usually obtained from a given park in a given year, and observations must be accumulated over time), 2) examining trends in bird populations and communities over time, and 3) exploring the relationships between bird species metrics and habitat variables.

I. Section A - Data Summary and Analysis

Bird Community Data Summaries

The bird community variables and indices selected for data summary purposes are descriptive and easily interpretable and will provide resource managers timely feedback to help assess management practices (Pickett et al. 1992). Prior to summary analysis, the resident status (permanent resident, summer resident, migrant) of each bird species recorded at a park is determined. Identification of the residency of each species is needed to exclude migrants from analysis of breeding birds within a park. The VCP is the unit of replication for analysis. Once estimates for all parameters have been obtained for each VCP, averages and standard deviations among VCPs can then be obtained for individual study units (management units or reference frames) or for park-wide inferences. Numbered subsections below reflect the order data summaries and analyses should be performed.

1) Individual Species Abundance and Frequency Summaries
Four measures are calculated: (1) The number of individuals of a species encountered per plot visit is calculated by dividing the total number of individuals of that species by the total number of plots visited. (2) The proportion of plots occupied by each species is calculated by dividing the total number of plots occupied by a species by the total number of plots visited. (3) Species density is generally determined by restricting the area of inference to a 100 m radius (3.14 ha) around each plot center, and dividing individuals observed on a plot by 3.14 ha. Distance 5.0 software (see section below), which accounts for un-detected individuals, should be used to estimate species densities if there are enough observations (~60) to do so accurately (Buckland et al. 1993, Buckland et al. 2001). (4) Local density is calculated using data only from plots where a species was encountered.

2) Species Diversity Analysis
Individual species abundance data are used to derive species diversity metrics at the VCP level. Where appropriate, all diversity metrics will be averaged at the study unit or park-wide level.

Species richness (S) is the total number of bird taxa recorded per VCP. Species richness is calculated with all resident species included in the estimate. Each report should include: (1) an appendix listing the number of resident individuals recorded on each plot, by species, and (2) a map showing species richness and the richness of species of continental importance, as determined by Partners in Flight (Rich et al. 2004), by plot.

The **Shannon diversity index** (H') is calculated for each VCP as:

$$H' = -\Sigma(n_i/N)\ln(n_i/N)$$

where n_1/N is the proportion of the total number of individuals in a population consisting of the ith species (Shannon 1949).

Species distribution evenness (J') is calculated by VCP according to Pielou J' (1977):

$$J' = H' / \ln(S)$$

where H' is the Shannon index and ln(S) is the maximum possible diversity for a given number of species if all species were present in equal numbers. Evenness is a measure of distribution of species within a community as compared to equal distribution and maximum diversity (Pielou 1969).

Shannon diversity index (H') can be partitioned into its basic components to look at whether changes in species composition (S) or species dominance (J') are driving the overall change in H' (Hayek and Buzas 1997):

$$H' = \ln(S) + \ln(J')$$

This provides insight into the underlying distribution of abundance among species within and among monitoring sites.

Habitat Data Summaries

Similar to the bird community data, habitat variables and indices selected for data summary purposes are descriptive and easily interpretable. Habitat data is collected on plots centered on each VCP monitoring locations. Once estimates for all parameters have been obtained for each plot, averages and standard deviations among plots can then be obtained for individual study units (management units or reference frames) or for park-wide inferences. Cover data, collected by class intervals, should be converted to median cover values prior to data summations and analysis (i.e., class 1 = 0.5, class 2 = 3.0, class 3 = 15.0, class 4 = 37.5, class 5 = 62.5, class 6 = 85.0, class 7 = 97.5). Numbered subsections below reflect the order data summaries and analyses should be performed.

1) 50-m Plot Data Analysis

Summary reports for habitat attributes at the 50-m radius plot level should be provided for "permanent" and "semi-permanent" features. For permanent features, a report should include a listing of the values for slope of plot, aspect of slope and topographic features. These values are measured only once and are assigned to a permanent locations table within the database. Semi-permanent plot features are not expected to change much, although features including percent cover of habitat types, road, and water are recorded each time a survey is conducted and should be reported.

2) 5-m Subplot Data Analysis

Like permanent attributes measured for plot locations, permanent features for subplots (i.e., azimuth, direction from plot center if more than one subplot is sampled; slope across subplot; and aspect of slope) are measured only once and stored in a separate table within the database. A report should include a listing of these values.

Tree Tally, a measure of stems per hectare is calculated as stems present per 0.00785 ha surveyed. Species are grouped to family and DBH size class (<1.0 cm, 1.1-2.5 cm, 2.6-8.0 cm, 8.1-15.0 cm, 15.1-38.0 cm and >38.0 cm) prior to calculating stems per hectare. Tree tallies illustrate size distribution of trees by family across a study unit or park. Knowing types and sizes of trees present serves as one measure for assessing habitat availability for forest bird species.

Woodland measures represent the forest structure in which a plot is located, and generally (but not always) denote a forested or riparian area. Woodland measures help delineate the habitat available for forest bird species. Canopy height in meters should be reported for hardwoods and conifers each time they are encountered on a plot. Canopy cover, recorded in the field as dots covered, should be converted to percent coverage (dot recorded x 1.04) before being reported.

Canopy cover is reported for deciduous trees, conifers, and total canopy coverage when encountered on a plot. Canopy cover is measured over plot center in the four cardinal directions. Therefore, canopy cover on a plot is determined by type by averaging the measures taken. Basal area summarizes tree density on a plot and is reported as m^2/ha. Basal area for a plot is determined by multiplying the stem count recorded on a field sheet for a plot by 2.5 for both hardwoods and conifers encountered.

The Horizontal Vegetation Profile represents the area obscured by vegetation, or screening cover for nesting birds, at various heights to 2 m. Values are reported for each height class (0 - 0.25, 0.25 - 0.5, 0.5 – 0.75, 0.75 - 1.0, 1.0 - 1.25, 1.25 -1.5, 1.5 – 1.75, and 1.75 - 2.0 m).

The Structural Diversity Index, a measure of vertical habitat available to birds, is calculated for each plot by summing the percents of possible touches (8 or 12) from vegetation (herbaceous, deciduous, and coniferous if present in a park) within each 1-m height increment, actually touched; dividing this value by the number of height increments measured (8); adding the resulting value to the percent of increments occupied; multiplying this value by 100; and then dividing it by two. Vertical structure diversity values were weighted to equally represent both the vertical height of vegetation and how dense the vegetation is within each height increment.

3) 1.78-m Subplot Data Analysis
Percent Ground Cover is a measure of non-vegetative attributes and includes bare soil, conifer litter, deciduous litter, grass litter, rock, unvegetated surface, and woody debris (>2.5 cm diameter). A report should include a listing of these values at the plot level as well as any values generated from summary analysis.

Percent Foliar Cover is a measure of vegetative cover recorded for cool season grass, forbs, moss and lichen, shrubs and vines, total vegetation cover (< 1.50 m), tree seedlings, and warm season grass plant guilds. A report should include a listing of these values at the plot level as well as any values generated from summary analysis.

II. Section B - Trend Analysis

Distance Analysis for Generating Bird Densities
Users should read two primary references for Distance 5.0: Buckland et al. 2001, "Introduction to Distance Sampling: Estimating abundance of biological populations" and Distance 5.0 "User's Guide". Additional information about Distance 5.0 software and supporting references may be obtained from the Distance website hosted by the Research Unit for Wildlife Population Assessment, University of St. Andrews, St. Andrews, Scotland at http://www.ruwpa.st-and.ac.uk/distance. Familiarity with Microsoft Access 2003 and the database Tweety7.0.mbd is needed in preparing data for transfer to Distance Software prior to analysis.

Preparing Bird Data for Export to Distance Software -- To determine distance calculations for population density estimates, data on species, flock-size, and distance are needed, all of which are located in tblBirdVCP. The data-summary-user-interface has a feature (1st option) that allows the creation of separate records for individuals based on flock-size. The second option, yields one record for each observation regardless of flock-size. The results are passed to a table

(1st option -- tblExportToDistance) or a query (2nd option – qryExportToDistance) which can be exported to Distance 5.0 software. Either way, the data will need to be cleaned up before it can be imported into Distance for analysis. Records with null values in the distance column or with null values in the flock-size column need to be removed. These represent either incomplete records (where distance estimation was not possible) or "flyovers" (individuals flying over the study area), and should be discarded from the Distance analysis. Details about data formatting prior to analysis are given in the following three sections.

Distance analysis is not limited to the output from the user-interface. Because each table in the database is linked by primary/foreign keys, you can create your own queries based on habitat type or management unit, flock size, and distance from observer in tblExportToDistance. Using certain habitat variables may lead to sample sizes that are too small for meaningful analysis. Procedures are given below to stratify bird abundance data by habitat types or study unit and to conduct the analysis. The following procedures describe how to transfer bird observation data and associated habitat data into Distance 5.0:

1) Custom Export from MS Access
1. Create the export table tblExportToDistance using the Data Summaries and Reports form.

2. Examine tblExportToDistance. Are there any habitat variables that you would like to add? In these procedures, we will create a query to link the riparian vs. upland field to the export data.

3. Close the table and go to Queries in the database container. Click on New. Select Okay for the Design view (see Figure 8.3). Add the table tblExportToDistance. Add the table tbl_Locations.

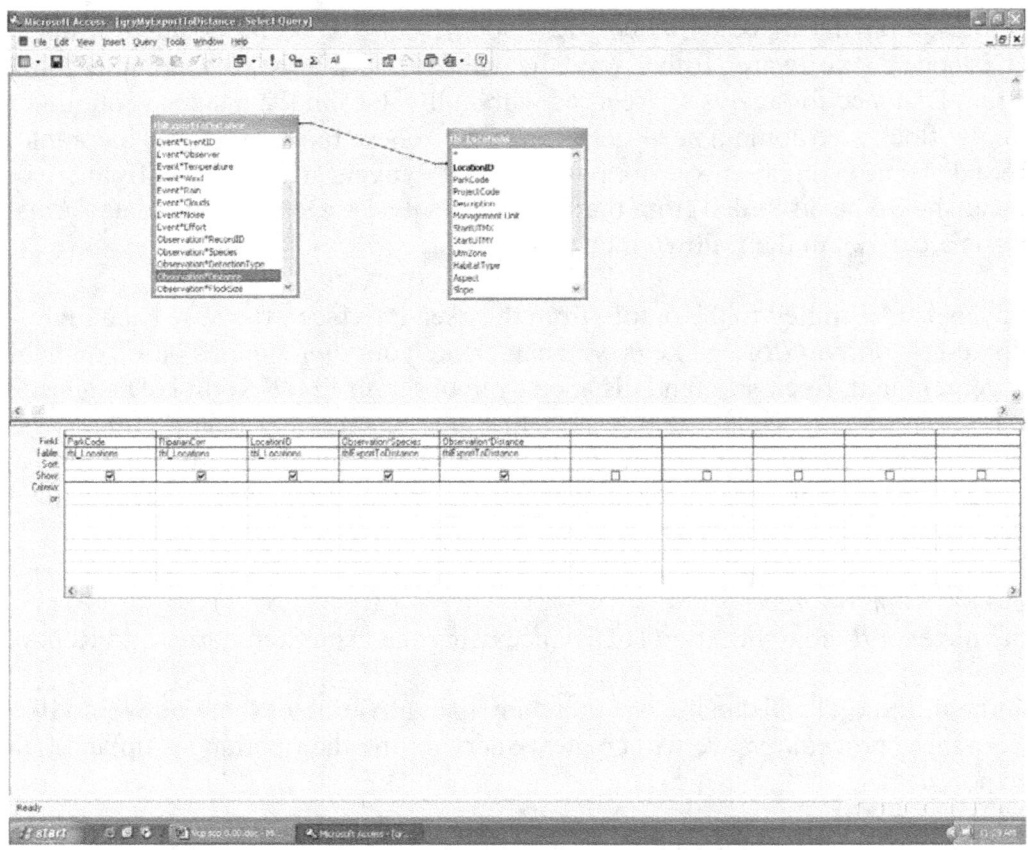

Figure 8.3. Creating a query in Design view for export to Distance 5.0.

4. Link the two tables in the upper window by dragging the field LocationsID from one table to the other. From tbl_Locations, select on the following fields by double-clicking on them: ParkCode, Riparian Plot, and LocationID. From tblExportToDistance, select on the following fields by double-clicking on them: Observation*Species and Observation*Distance.

5. Click the "save" icon on the upper left corner of the window and name the query "qryMyExportToDistance".

6. We are now ready to export the data. Go to "File → Save As/Export…" Choose Save To an External File or Database. Under file type, select Text Files. Click on the Export button. You now have a choice of using delimiters or using fixed width form. You will probably want to clean up the data in a spreadsheet before importing it into Distance. For example, you may want to analyze data for just a single species at one park. All of this can be accomplished from within Access or using a spreadsheet such as Excel. If you do create new export tables from Access, be sure to work with back-up copies of tables.

Importing into Distance 5.0 -- There are many ways to stratify point transect data as it is imported into Distance. In this example the data could be stratified as:

Data Layer	Field Name
Study Area	Park
Region	Riparian Plot
Point Transect	LocationID
Observation	Distance

The example is for Red-winged Blackbirds, which occur in both riparian and prairie habitats at Tallgrass Prairie National Preserve and Agate Fossil Beds National Monument, but at very different densities. For convenience, the import file should be tab-delimited text with the fields from right to left sorted ascending. Fields include: park, riparian plot, locationID and distance. This is easy to do with a spreadsheet such as MS Excel. Start Distance 5.0 and follow the procedures as follows:

2) New Project Wizard
1. Create a new project with the icon in the upper left window. For example, RWBL_Prairie. In the next window (Step 1) select I want to: analyze a survey that has been completed. Click on Next.

2. Step 2, reviews your choices and the basic data structure.

3. Step 3, make the following choices: Type of survey – point transect; accept all other (default) selections on this window. Click on Next.

4. Step 4, accept the default units of measure (meters, hectares). Click on Next.

5. Step 5, do not select multipliers. Leave these boxes blank. Click Next.

6. Under Step 6, choose Destinations: Proceed to Data Import Wizard.

3) Data Import Wizard
1. Step 1, is an introduction to the data import process. Click Next.

2. Step 2, select the text file you are importing into Distance. Click on Next.

3. Step 3, data destination. Use default destination settings. Click on Next.

4. Step 4, at this point, the Distance software is attempting to look at your data. The default delimiter is tab. If you used comma, semicolon or space, indicate that here.

5. Step 5, you now can label columns in the data (Figure 8.4).

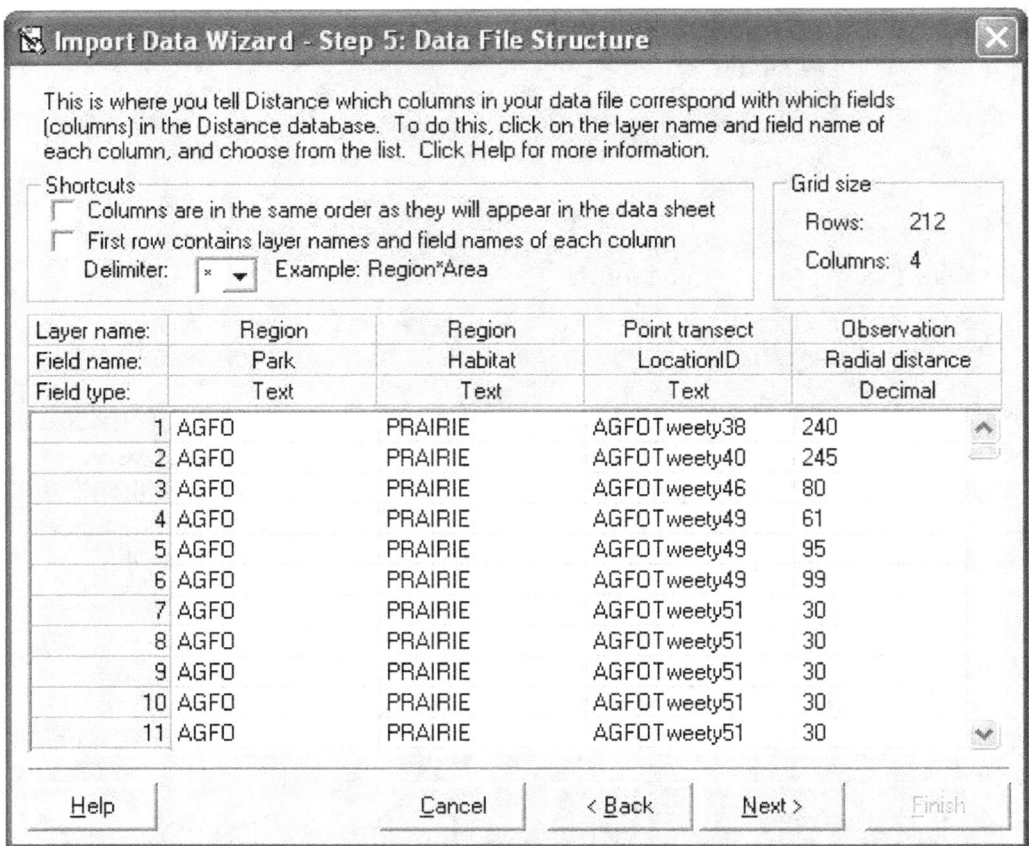

Figure 8.4. Importing bird distance data into Distance 5.0. Step 5 of the Import Data Wizard is to identify the data file structure including field names.

6. Step 6, ends the import procedure. You may choose to overwrite existing data or add to existing data. The default is to overwrite, which we accept here. Click on Finish. At this point the data will be loading into Distance 5.0

7. Click on the Data folder to confirm that your data are actually in Distance 5.0. Click on the binoculars. The entire data structure should appear including study area, region, point transect and observation (see Figure 8.5).

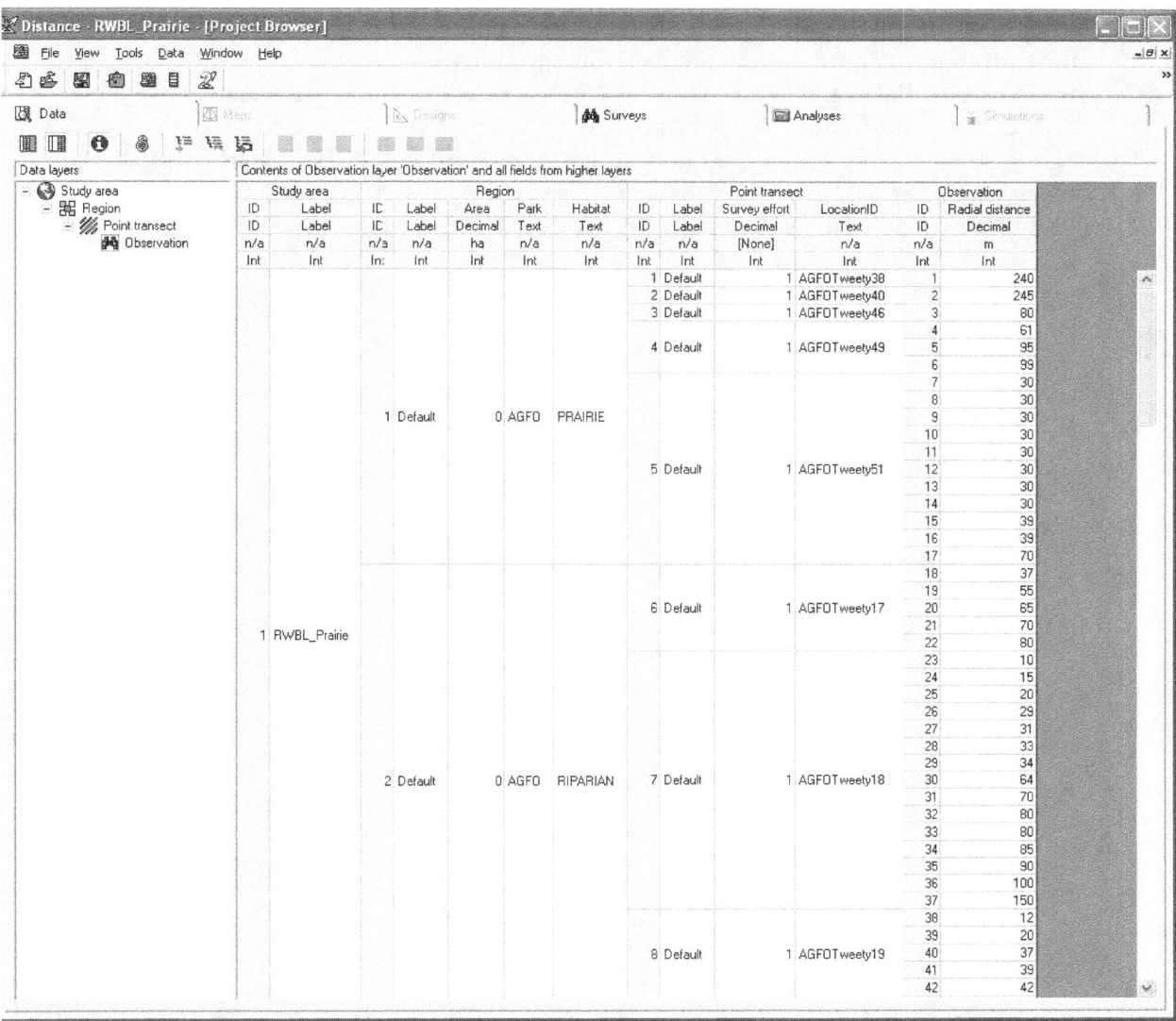

Figure 8.5. Data screen in Distance 5.0 with Red-winged Blackbird distance values at Agate Fossil Beds National Monument.

4) Analysis

1. With a sample of bird abundance survey data in Distance 5.0, we are now ready to look at the status of Red-wing Blackbird populations at Agate Fossil Beds National Monument and Tallgrass Prairie National Preserve.

2. Select the analysis tab from the upper portion of the window. Select Analysis, Analysis Details from the Menu at the top of the window. To try out the software with a preliminary analysis using the default distance models, click Run.

3. The analysis run will generate three tab windows. The Inputs window provides information about which data set was run, and which model was used in the analysis. The log provides information about the analysis run that might include warnings such as critical assumption violations and how the software is addressing them. The output

results contain descriptions about the data and models being used in the analysis, a glossary of terms used in the models (which is really nice!!), model parameter values used to fit the data, graphical output of the distance distribution (note: you will have to click on the Next button, to get through all of the output), and goodness-of-fit tests. Again, software users are urged to become very familiar with Buckland et al. (2001), which describes the theory and gives a number of real-world examples. There is also a list-serve available to discuss application of the theory or use of the software.

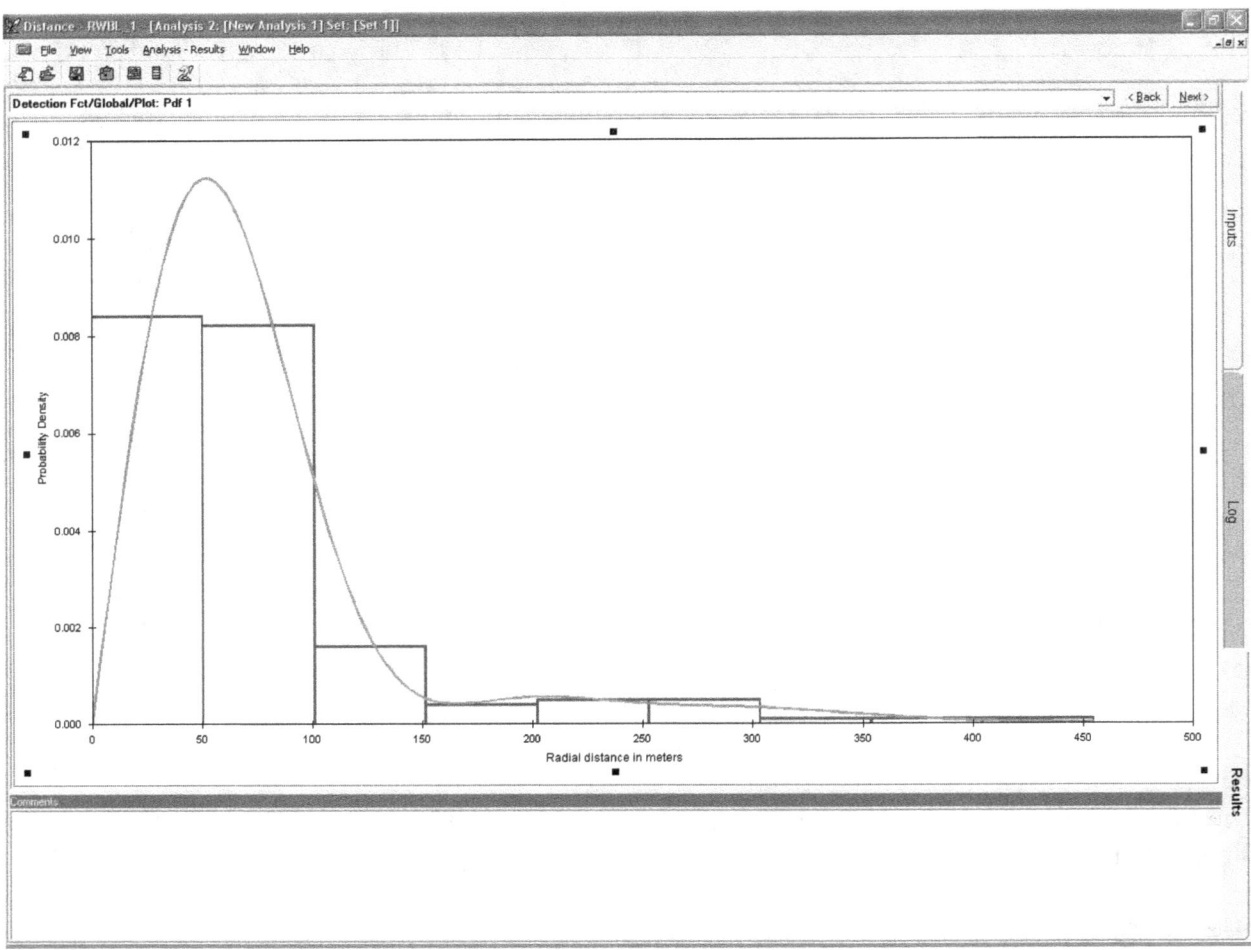

Figure 8.6 Distance distribution for Red-winged Blackbird for all observations pooled.

Detecting changes in bird populations

Many analytic methods have been used in attempts to detect change in bird populations (e.g., Hatfield et al. 1996, Thomas 1996), and the best technique will ultimately depend upon various aspects of the sample design. The first step in any trend analysis will be to plot the data (e.g., abundance of a bird species or a diversity measure) as a function of time. Visual inspection of such plots may reveal important changes, and may also be useful in detecting potential outliers in preparation for formal statistical tests.

A simple linear regression is frequently as powerful or more powerful than other similar techniques (Hatfield et al. 1996). It should be kept in mind, however, that regressions do not test for trend *per se*; they evaluate how well the data fit a specified function. Thus, the first step is to visually examine scatter plots of data for the most appropriate regression function. Linear regression will usually provide the best fit, but curvilinear and piecewise models should also be considered. See Kutner et al. (2005) for an in-depth treatment of regression models.

Because *P*-values are dependent on sample size, and each park will be sampled only once every four years, several decades will elapse before the *t*-test statistic associated with simple regression analyses obtains much statistical power. Thus, in the shorter term, the most informative approach to a regression analysis is likely to be estimation of regression parameters (e.g., the slope, which is indicative of the rate of change), rather than determination of statistical significance. In other words, focus should be on whether the measured changes are biologically important, rather than statistically significant (see Morrison 2007). If statistical significance is computed for more than one simple regression analysis, then the issue of multiple comparisons must be dealt with (see below).

Another option to change detection is a control chart approach in which the abundance of a bird or a diversity measure is plotted as a function of time, along with a threshold or thresholds that indicate the need for management action. Such thresholds may be set by statistical criteria, but may also need to be determined by management goals or other subjective criteria. (See Morrison 2008 for a discussion of control charts.)

Habitat relationships
To better understand breeding bird-habitat relationships, several approaches are possible, depending upon the information desired.

The first step in any analysis of habitat data will be to carefully evaluate each habitat variable for each park. Not all habitat variables will be informative for a given park (or study unit; Appendix D). Nor will most habitat variables appear to be derived from a normal distribution (Appendix D), which is necessary for most statistical analyses. Usually, only a small subset of habitat variables should be chosen for any given analysis; these should represent habitat attributes that are known to be important for the bird species of interest, or are of interest to park management.

One may be interested in making spatial comparisons among sites across a park (or study unit) at one point in time; in this case each sample site would represent a replicate. Alternatively, one may be interested in temporal comparisons for a given park (or study unit); in this case all sample sites would be averaged and each sampling occasion would represent a replicate. This latter approach is indicated by the protocol objective of "correlating changes in bird community composition and abundance with changes in habitat variables", although the first approach could be employed if interest exists in such 'snapshot' spatial comparisons.

1) Univariate analyses
If interest is on determining how a specific habitat variable is associated with the abundance of a given bird species or some diversity measure, it is possible to evaluate a simple pairwise correlation between the habitat variable and bird metric. A Pearson correlation coefficient can be calculated if both variables appear to be from a normal distribution, otherwise a Spearman

correlation coefficient should be used (or the appropriate transformations applied to normalize the distributions).

If interest is on determining whether a given habitat variable is associated with the presence or absence of a species, a simple logistic regression could be employed. Logistic regression does not require that the predictor variable come from a normal distribution.

If more than one simple pairwise correlation or simple logistic regression is calculated from the same data set, and inferences regarding statistical significance are desired, the probability of a Type I error will change accordingly, depending upon how many comparisons are made simultaneously. There does not exist general agreement on the best way to deal with such multiple comparisons in relation to Type I error (e.g., Perneger 1998, Cabin and Mitchell 2000, Moran 2003, Nakagawa 2004). A conservative approach is to report actual P-values from each individual test, and indicate which of these would still be significant after correction for multiple comparisons by a method such as the sequential Bonferroni technique (Rice 1989).

2) Multivariate analyses
Multiple habitat variables could be combined in the same analysis with a multivariate approach. Many of the habitat variables will not appear to come from a normal distribution, however, and this violates the assumptions of many multivariate analyses. Moreover, because of the relatively small sample size (number of sites) at most parks, relatively few habitat variables could be included in a given analysis in a spatial comparison, and many sampling events over time would be necessary for temporal comparisons (See Appendix D for a discussion of minimum sample size). Finally, many of the habitat variables will be strongly intercorrelated. Thus, the best strategy for any multivariate analysis will be to select a small subset of habitat variables that are likely to be informative (as discussed above) and with relatively weak intercorrelations. If such variables do not appear to be from a normal distribution, and the analysis requires it, transformations will be necessary.

One option in dealing with a large number of predictive variables in multivariate analyses is to use a factor analysis method (e.g., principle components analysis) to reduce the dimensionality of the problem, resulting in a smaller set of derived variables. There are two disadvantages to this approach with this breeding bird data set: (1) The sample sizes necessary (10 per habitat variable to 300 overall; MacCallum et al. 1999) will be larger than the sample sizes usually available. (2) The resulting "derived" variables will likely be more difficult for resource managers to interpret or manage. Thus the best strategy will usually be to select a small subset of actual habitat variables prior to any analysis, as described above.

If interest is on determining how various habitat variables are associated with the abundance of a given bird species or some diversity measure, a multiple linear regression could be employed. If interest is on determining how various habitat variables are associated with the presence or absence of a given species, a multiple logistic regression could be employed. As long as the habitat variables of interest are specified beforehand (and are not too numerous in relation to the sample size), these procedures are relatively straightforward.

If, on the other hand, the goal is model selection (i.e., choosing the 'best' subset of predictors from a larger set of variables), various techniques are available. A stepwise approach to multiple regression has often been employed in this context. Stepwise procedures have been increasingly criticized, however (e.g., Mac Nally 2000, Whittingham et al. 2006), and the information theoretic approach is frequently advocated as a superior alternative. Akaike's Information Criterion (AIC) is an information theoretic technique that is widely used to select the 'best' model from a set of competing models (Burnham and Anderson 2002).

Thus, if model selection is the goal, AIC is the preferred alternative. A stepwise method may be useful in some cases, however, the analyst should realize the issues surrounding this approach (e.g., Whittingham et al. 2006). Both procedures are sufficiently complex that they are beyond the scope of this SOP to describe. See Hosmer and Lemeshow (2000) and Harrell (2001) for discussion of regression approaches and (Burnham and Anderson 2002) for a discussion of the AIC technique. The analyst should pay particular attention to minimal sample sizes necessary in relation to the number of habitat variables in the model. There is a "small sample AIC" statistic that can be used for small sample sizes (Burnham and Anderson 2002). Models created by a model selection method for a particular park in a given year should be considered as "predictive" models (e.g., MacNally 2000), and data from subsequent years used to test the predictions (i.e., for spatial comparisons).

Breeding Bird Monitoring Protocol for the Heartland Network Inventory and Monitoring Program

Standard Operation Procedure 9: Reporting

Version 2.00 (05/09/2008)

Revision History Log:

Previous Version #	Revision Date	Author	Changes Made	Reason for Change	New Version #

This SOP gives step-by-step instructions for reporting on variable circular plot bird count and habitat survey data collected by Heartland Network Inventory and Monitoring Program (HTLN). The SOP describes the procedure for formatting a report, the review process and distribution of completed reports. Efficient reporting on monitoring results is critical in assisting park Resource Managers in management decisions. Therefore, a reporting schedule is given with critical dates identified.

I. Report Format

Template

The report template for Natural Resource Technical Reports should be followed (http://www.nature.nps.gov/publications/NRPM/index.cfm). Natural resource reports are the designated medium for disseminating high priority, current natural resource management information with managerial application. The Natural Resource Technical Reports series is used to disseminate the peer-reviewed results of scientific studies in the physical, biological, and social sciences for both the advancement of science and the achievement of the National Park Service's mission.

Style

Standards for scientific writing as recommended in the CBE Style Manual (CBE Style Manual Committee 1994) should be followed. Reports should be direct and concise. Refer also to Mack (1986), Goldwasser (1999), Day and Gastel (2006), and Strunk and White (2000) for guidelines on appropriate writing style.

II. Types of Reports and Review Process

Table 9.1 summarizes the types of reports produced and review process. Adapted from DeBacker et al. 2005.

Type of Report	Purpose of Report	Primary Audience	Review Process	Frequency
Comprehensive 4 - year Status Reports	Summarize monitoring data collected during a sampling year by HTLN and any observations made by park staff and volunteers during the previous three years, to provide an update on the status of avian communities and their habitat. Document related data management activities and data summaries.	Park resource managers and external scientists	Internal peer review by HTLN staff	Every 4th year
Executive Summary of Comprehensive 4 - year Status Reports	Same as Comprehensive 4 – year Status Reports but summarized to highlight key points for non-technical audiences.	Superintendents, interpreters, and the general public	Internal peer review by HTLN staff	Simultaneous with Comprehensive 4 - year Status Reports
Comprehensive Trends and Analysis and Synthesis Reports	Describe and interpret trends in avian communities and their habitat. Describe and interpret relationships among observed trends and park management, known stressors, climate, etc. Highlight resources of concern that may require management action.	Park resource managers and external scientists	Internal peer review by HTLN staff	Every 12 -16 years
Executive Summary of Comprehensive Trends and Analysis and Synthesis Reports	Same as Comprehensive Trends and Analysis and Synthesis Reports, but summarized to highlight findings and recommendations for non-technical audiences.	Superintendents, interpreters, and the general public	Internal peer review by HTLN staff	Simultaneous with Comprehensive Trends Analysis and Synthesis Reports

III. Report Distribution

Following review, the comprehensive report for a park will be distributed to the resource management staff and the superintendent by March 31st of the year after data is collected by the HTLN. Reports can also be distributed to interested partners involved in conservation of avian resources. This determination is made by the park, the network, or the regional office. All data collected is public property and subject to requests under the Freedom of Information Act (FOIA). However, sensitive data, such as the location of rare species, must be withheld in some cases. Reports containing non-sensitive data will be made publicly available and disseminated through the network website: **(http://www1.nature.nps.gov/im/units/htln/index.htm)**.

Breeding Bird Monitoring Protocol for the Heartland Network Inventory and Monitoring Program

Standard Operation Procedure 10: Procedures and Equipment Storage After the Field Season

Version 2.00 (05/09/2008)

Revision History Log:

Previous Version #	Revision Date	Author	Changes Made	Reason for Change	New Version #

This Standard Operating Procedure explains procedures that all field observers using the Breeding Bird Monitoring Protocol for the Heartland Network Inventory and Monitoring Program (HTLN) should be familiar with and follow after the field season is completed.

I. Procedure

Clean and repair all equipment prior to returning to proper storage areas in the HTLN building or the HTLN storage building. All reference manuals should be re-shelved on their appropriate bookshelf. Other reference materials and extra data sheets need to be filed in their appropriate filing cabinet. Clean the insides and outsides of all vehicles used in the field.

Organize field data sheets and check that they have been filled out completely. As a rule, all data sheets need to be reviewed for completeness before the crew leaves the field. However, because of the number of field days and crewmembers, some deficiencies in data recording may not be identified until all data sheets have been organized and reviewed as a group (e.g. when habitat work has inadvertently been missed for a plot).

Identify and obtain ancillary data. It is of critical importance that this data be incorporated into the bird monitoring efforts. First and foremost, knowledge of management efforts in a park for that year (i.e. controlled burns and cattle grazing) will be used to assess the effects of these efforts on the habitat and birds present. Second, vegetation data collected by HTLN will assist in evaluating habitat types and may give an indication as to why the presence or absence of a bird species was observed. Certain plants may be utilized for food, cover or nesting differently by different birds, thus altering the bird communities observed. Climate can also influence bird numbers, both directly and indirectly. Excess precipitation can disrupt nesting success while drought conditions may limit plant growth, thus food and cover availability for young. Therefore, annual climate data will be obtained from a region-wide climatic database on the internet at: http://ag3.agebb.missouri.edu/npsdata/.

At the end of each field trip, file a trip report with the data manager outlining hours worked, field-crew members and their responsibilities on the project, and any unique situations encountered. This information is incorporated in the database and used during data analysis. This information is critical for identifying causes for discrepancies and inconsistencies in the data. The project manager is responsible for filing all trip reports.

Breeding Bird Monitoring Protocol for the Heartland Network Inventory and Monitoring Program

Standard Operation Procedure 11: Revising the Protocol

Version 2.00 (05/09/2008)

Revision History Log:

Previous Version #	Revision Date	Author	Changes Made	Reason for Change	New Version #

This Standard Operating Procedure explains how to make changes to the Narrative of the Breeding Bird Monitoring Protocol for the Heartland Network Inventory and Monitoring Program (HTLN) and accompanying SOPs, and tracking these changes. Observers asked to edit the Protocol Narrative or any one of the SOPs need to follow this outlined procedure to eliminate confusion in how data is collected and analyzed. All observers should be familiar with this SOP to identify and use the most current methodologies.

I. Procedures:

1. The Breeding Bird Monitoring Protocol Narrative for HTLN and accompanying SOPs has attempted to incorporate the most sound methodologies for collecting and analyzing bird data. However, all protocols regardless of how sound require editing as new and different information becomes available. Required edits should be made in a timely manner and appropriate reviews undertaken.

2. All edits require review for clarity and technical soundness. Small changes or additions to existing methods will be reviewed in-house by HTLN staff. However, if a complete change in methods is sought, than an outside review is required. Regional and National staff of the National Park Service with familiarity in avian research and data analysis will be utilized as reviewers. Also, experts in avian research and statistical methodologies outside of the Park Service will be utilized in the review process.

3. Document edits and protocol versioning in the Revision History Log that accompanies the Protocol Narrative and each SOP. Log changes in the Protocol Narrative or SOP being edited only. Version numbers increase incrementally by hundredths (e.g. version 1.01, version 1.02, …etc) for minor changes. Major revisions should be designated with the next whole number (e.g., version 2.0, 3.0,…etc). Record the previous version number, date of revision, author of the revision, identify paragraphs and pages where

changes are made, and the reason for making the changes along with the new version number.

4. Inform the Data Manager about changes to the Protocol Narrative or SOP so the new version number can be incorporated in the Metadata of the project database. The database may have to be edited by the Data Manager to accompany changes in the Protocol Narrative and SOPs.

5. Post new versions on the internet and forward copies to all individuals with a previous version of the affected Protocol Narrative or SOP.

10. Appendix

Appendix A. Park maps with bird plot locations

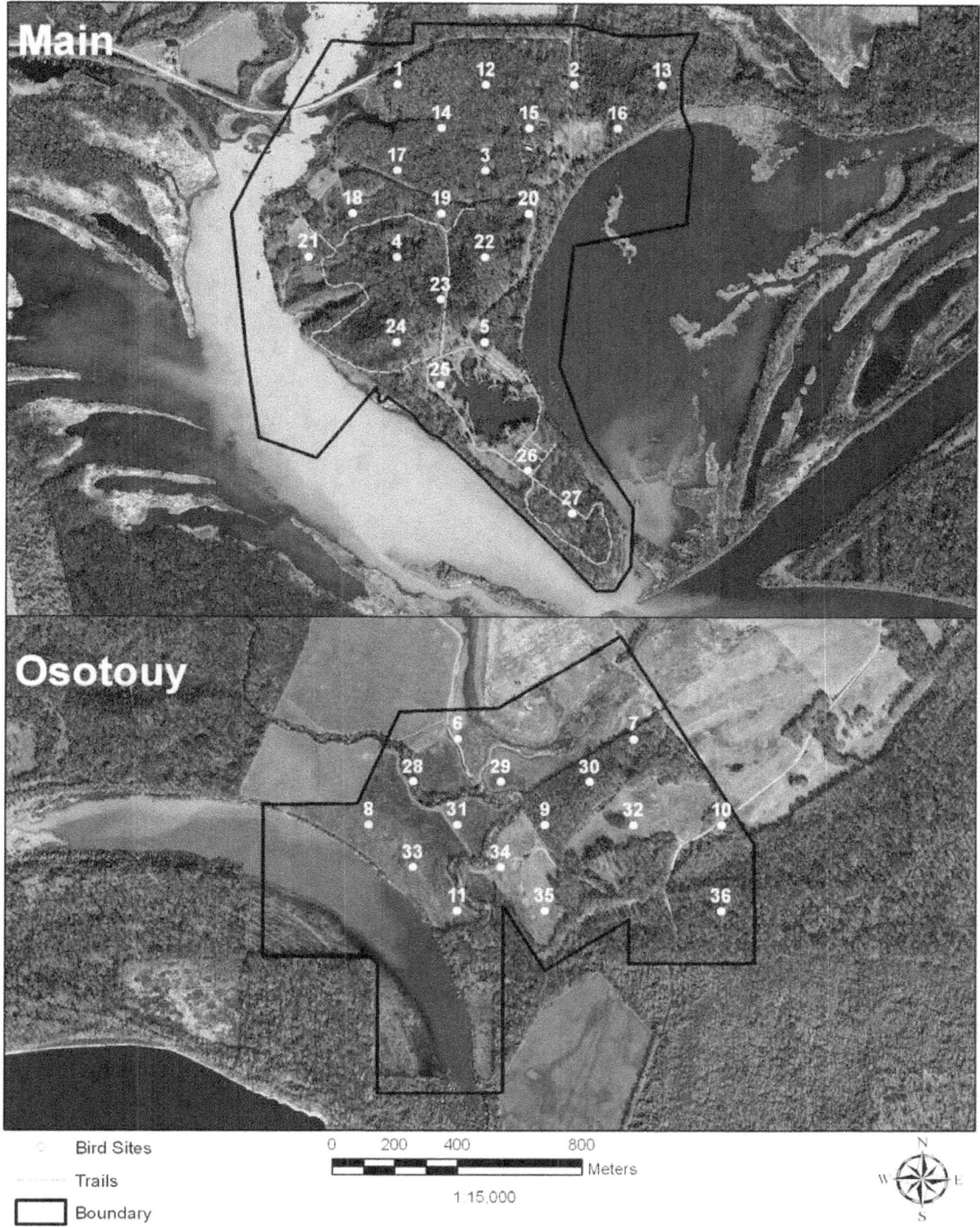

Figure A.1. Heartland Network Bird Monitoring Sites at Arkansas Post National Memorial, Arkansas.

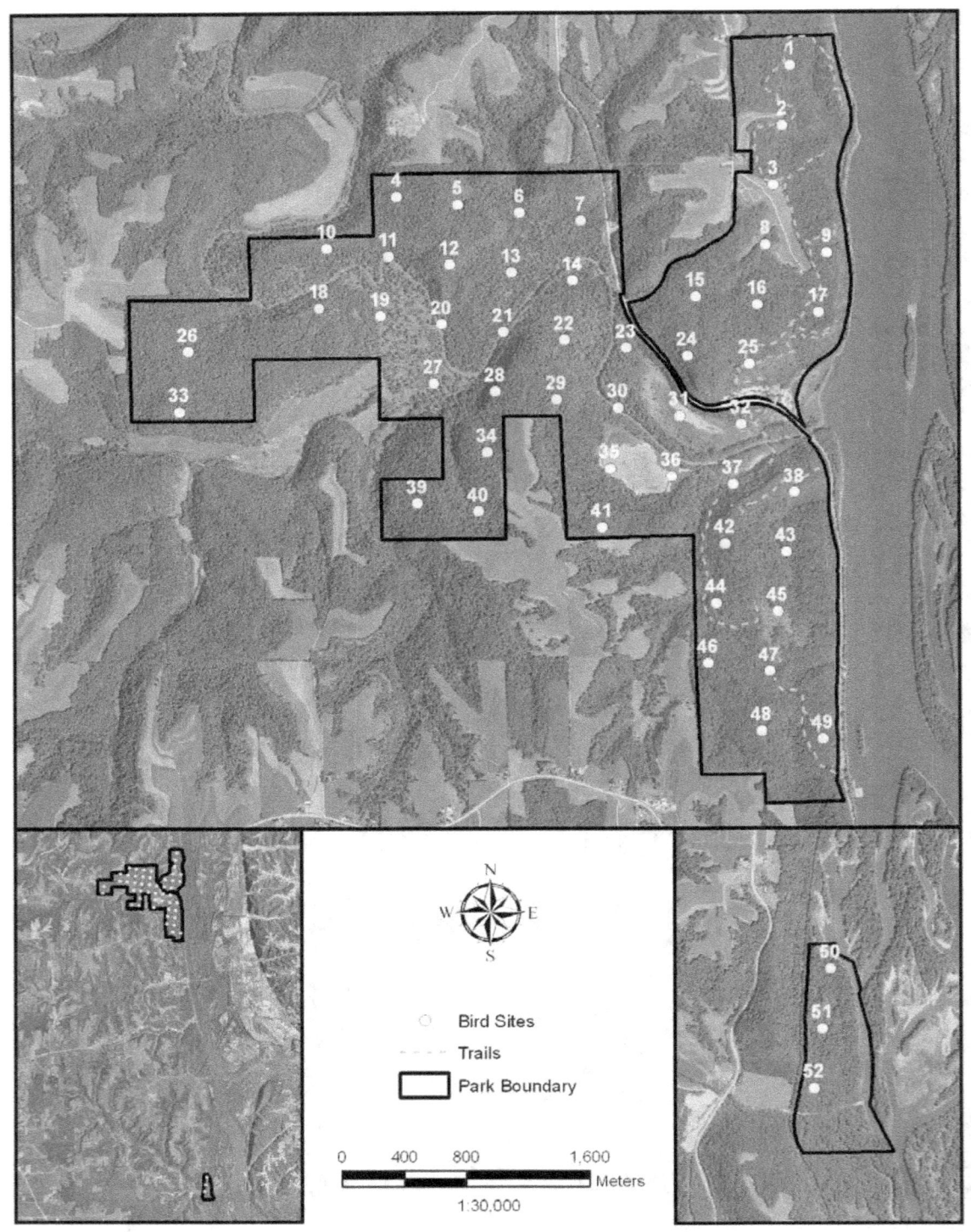

Figure A.2. Heartland Network Bird Monitoring Sites at Effigy Mounds National Monument, Iowa.

Figure A.3. Heartland Network Bird Monitoring Sites at George Washington Carver National Monument, Missouri.

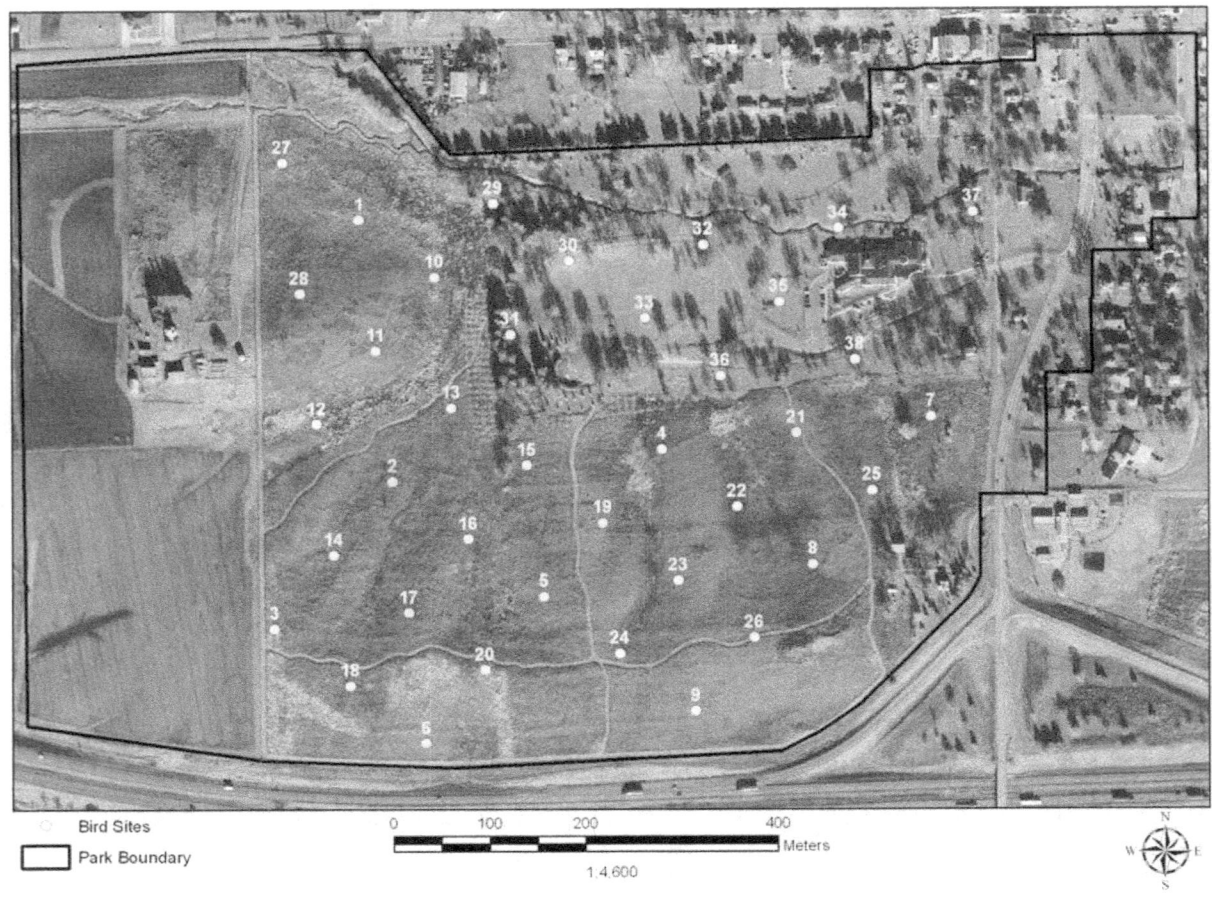

Figure A.4. Heartland Network Bird Monitoring Sites at Herbert Hoover National Historic Site, Iowa.

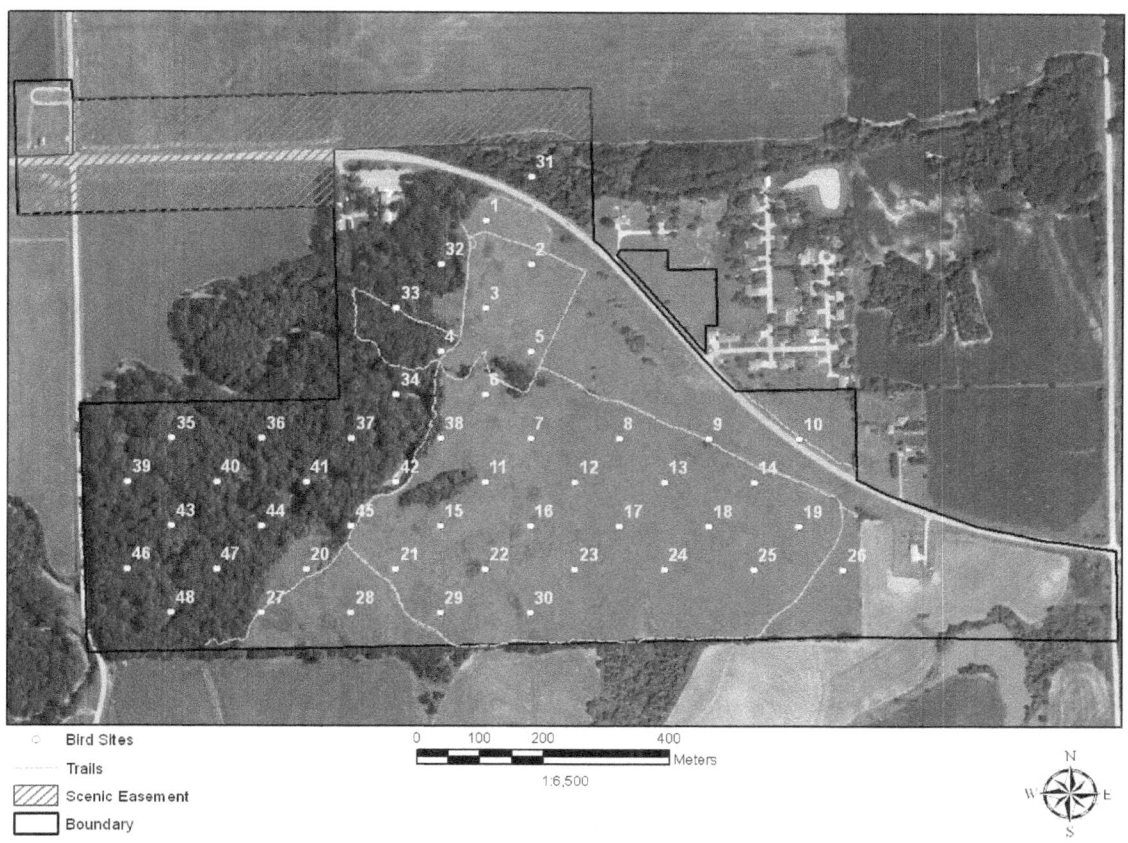

Figure A.5. Heartland Network Bird Monitoring Sites at Homestead National Monument of America, Nebraska.

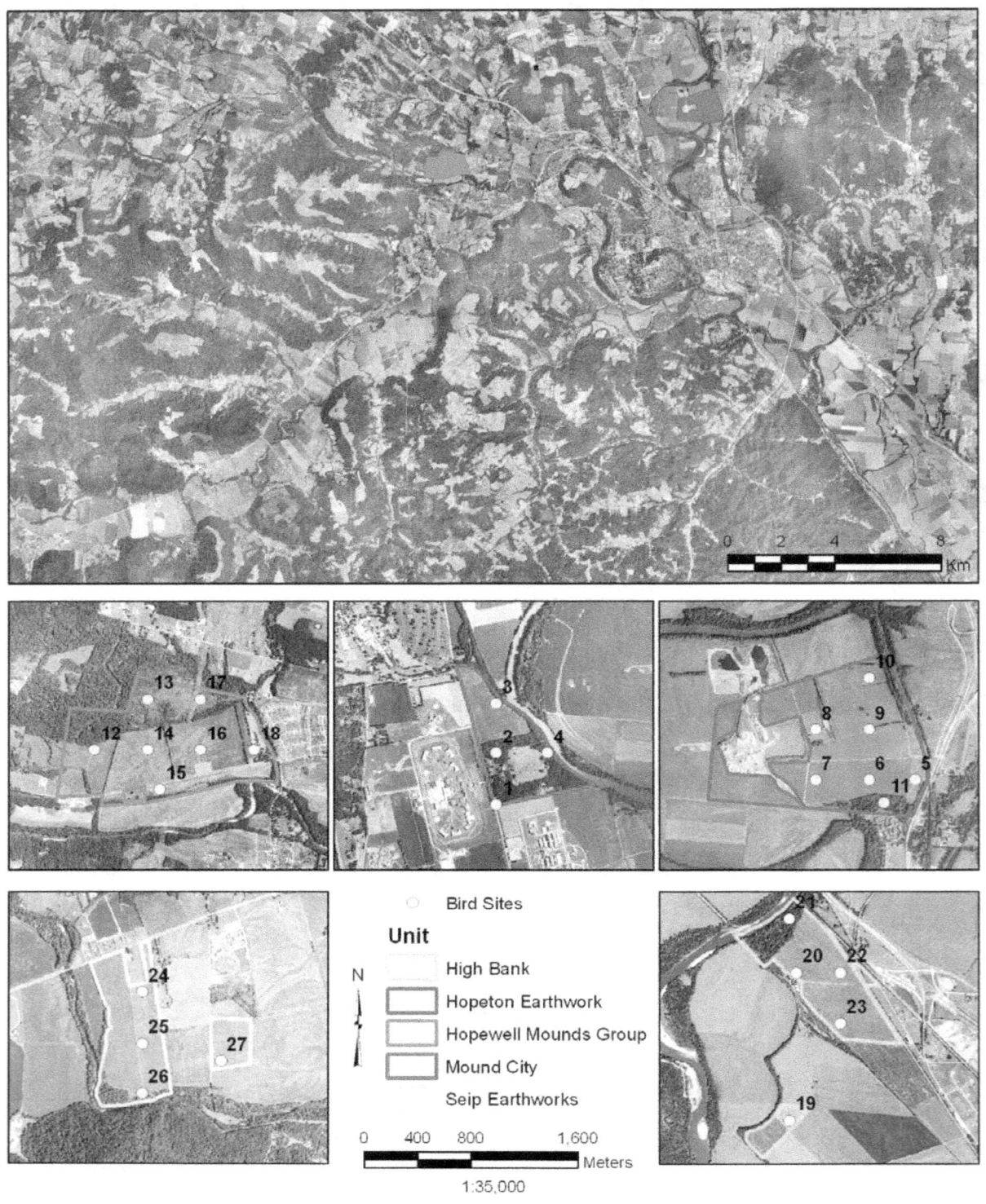

Figure A.6. Heartland Network Bird Monitoring Sites at Hopewell Culture National Historical Site, Ohio.

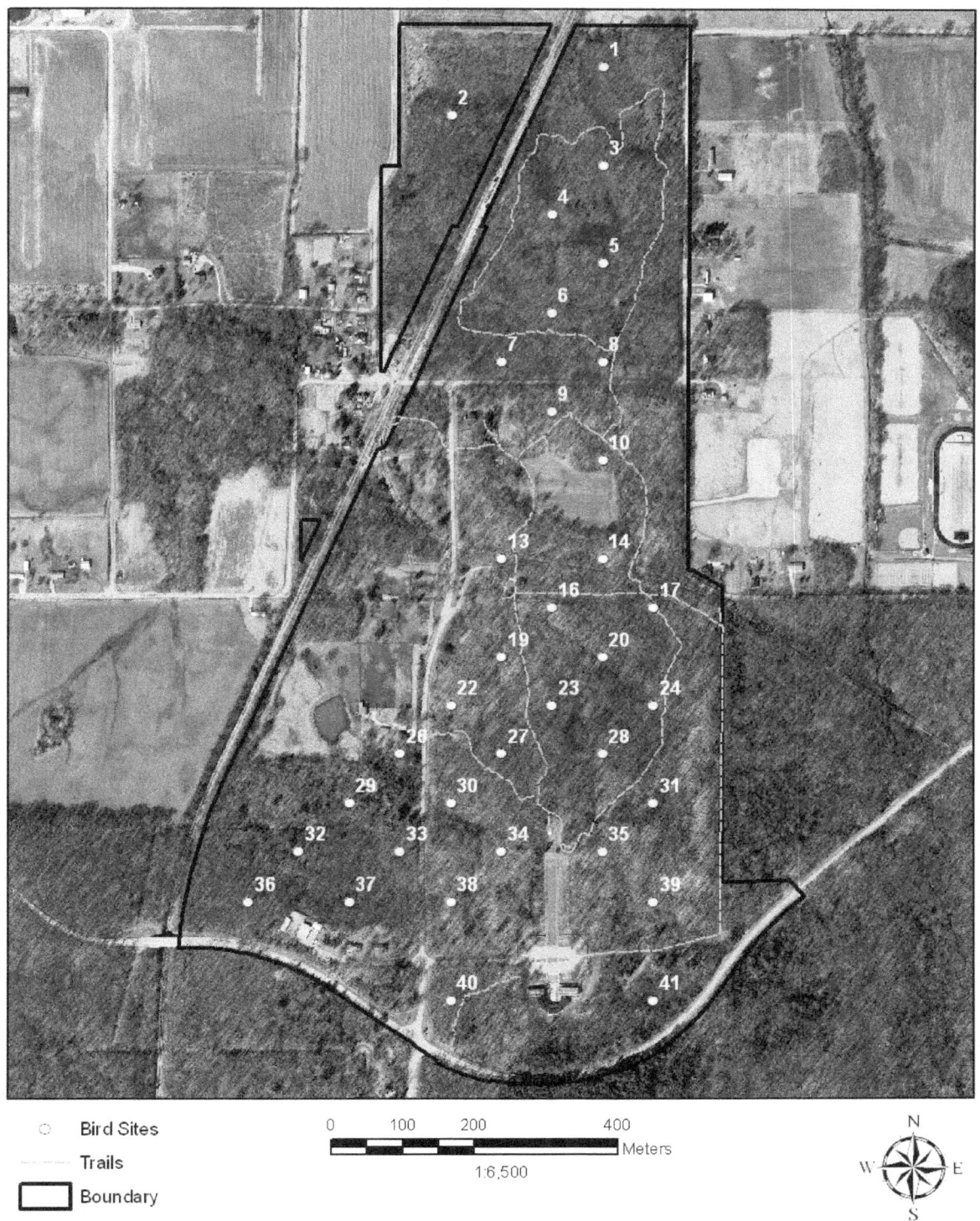

Figure A.7. Heartland Network Bird Monitoring Sites at Lincoln Boyhood National Memorial, Indiana.

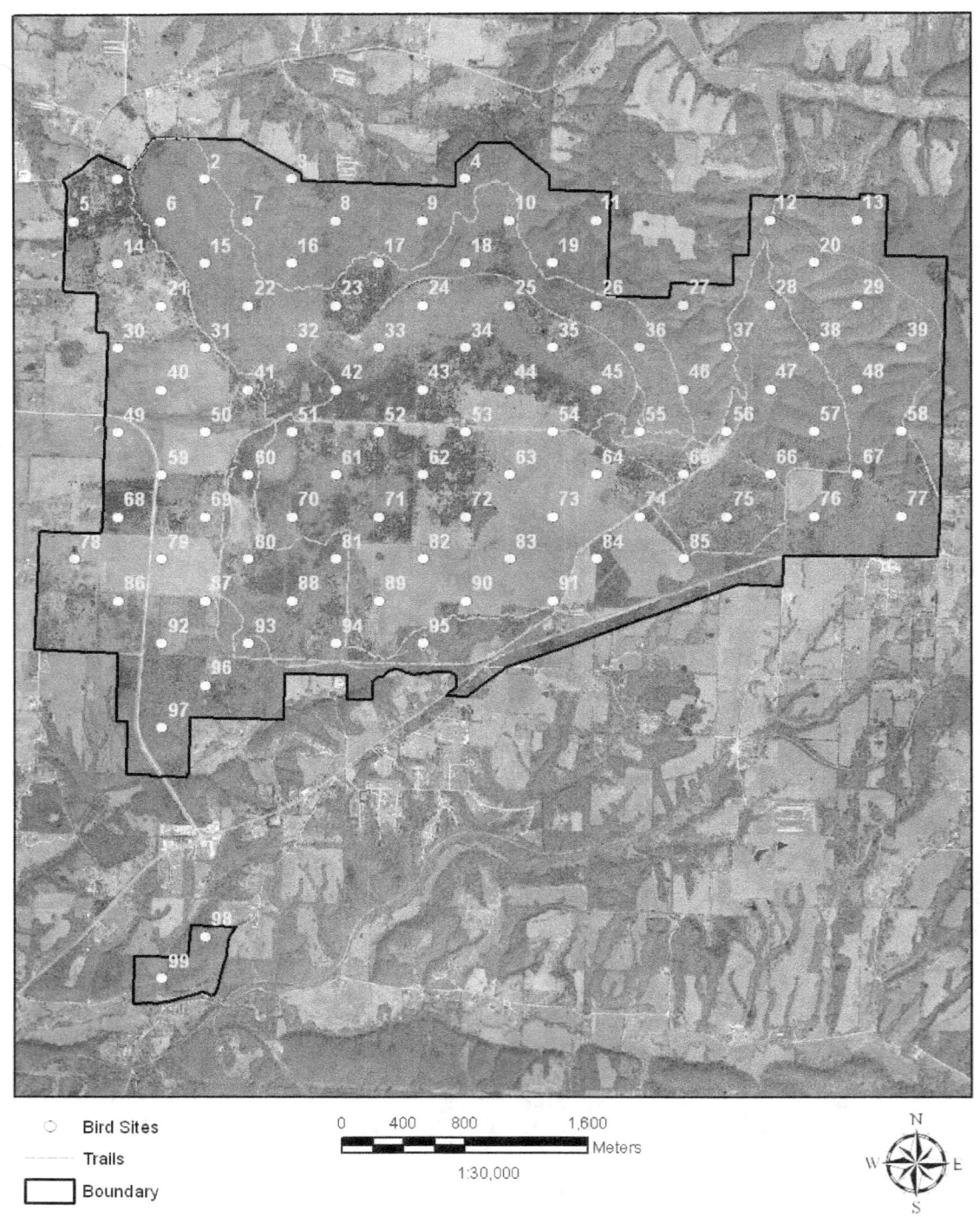

Figure A.8. Heartland Network Bird Monitoring Sites at Pea Ridge National Military Park, Arkansas.

Figure A.9. Heartland Network Bird Monitoring Sites at Pipestone National Monument, Minnesota.

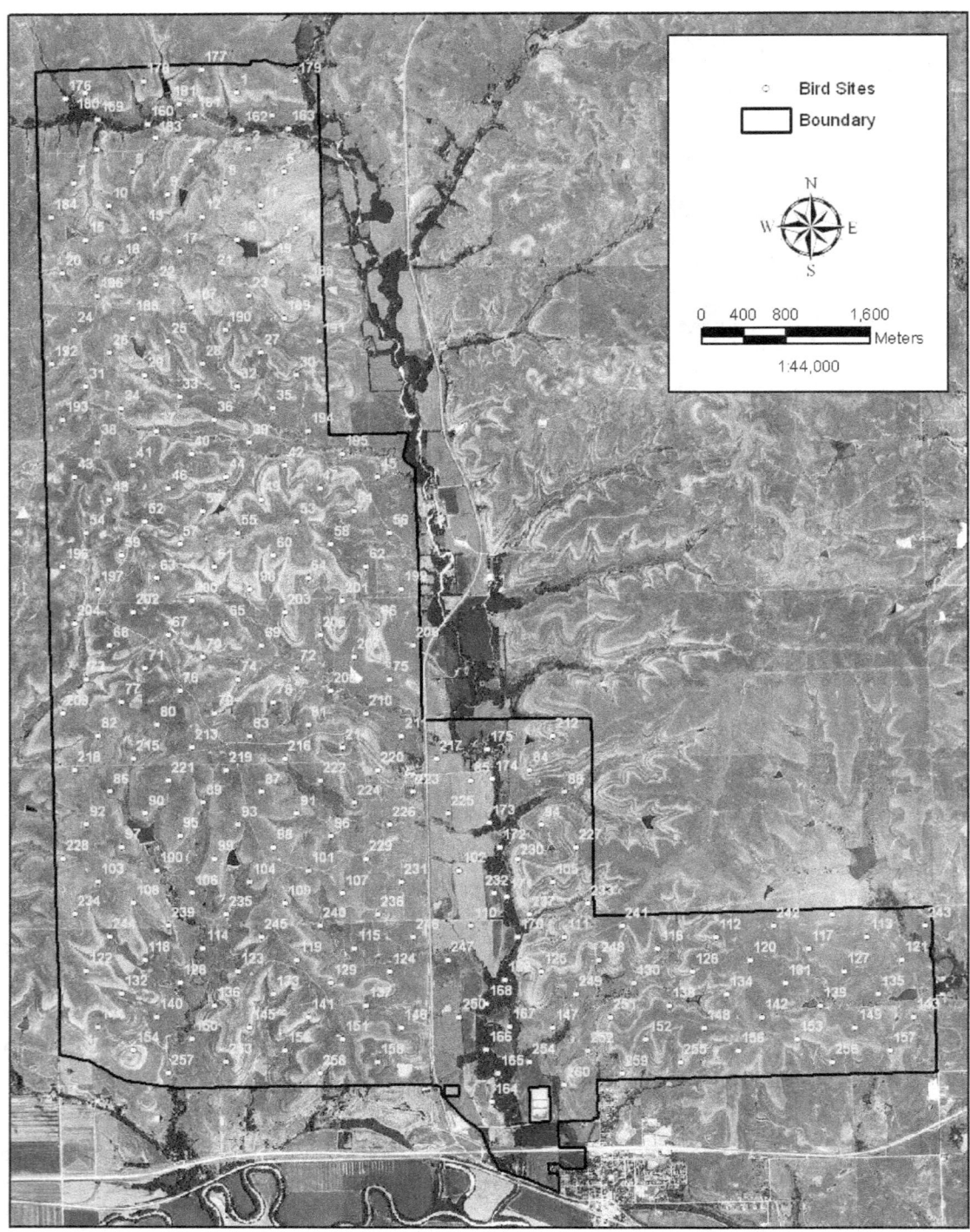

Figure A.10. Heartland Network Bird Monitoring Sites at Tallgrass Prairie National Preserve, Kansas.

Figure A.11. Heartland Network Bird Monitoring Sites at Wilson's Creek National Battlefield, Missouri.

Appendix B. Waypoints for Heartland Network Bird Monitoring Sites, by Park

Table B.1: Waypoints for Arkansas Post National Memorial, Arkansas - UTM Zone 15 North Datum 1983 (Conus).

Plot I.D	X Coordinate (Easting)	Y Coordinate (Northing)	Inventory I.D. Number
ARPOTweety1	652413.656	3766221.835	ARPO_1
ARPOTweety2	652979.342	3766221.835	ARPO_2
ARPOTweety3	652696.499	3765938.992	ARPO_3
ARPOTweety4	652413.656	3765656.149	ARPO_4
ARPOTweety5	652696.499	3765373.306	ARPO_5
ARPOTweety6	660050.410	3761979.194	ARPO_6
ARPOTweety7	660616.095	3761979.194	ARPO_7
ARPOTweety8	659767.567	3761696.351	ARPO_8
ARPOTweety9	660333.252	3761696.351	ARPO_9
ARPOTweety10	660898.938	3761696.351	ARPO_10
ARPOTweety11	660050.410	3761413.508	ARPO_11
ARPOTweety12	652696.499	3766221.835	ARPO_12
ARPOTweety13	653262.184	3766221.835	ARPO_13
ARPOTweety14	652555.078	3766080.413	ARPO_14
ARPOTweety15	652837.920	3766080.413	ARPO_15
ARPOTweety16	653120.763	3766080.413	ARPO_16
ARPOTweety17	652413.656	3765938.992	ARPO_17
ARPOTweety18	652272.235	3765797.571	ARPO_18
ARPOTweety19	652555.078	3765797.571	ARPO_19
ARPOTweety20	652837.920	3765797.571	ARPO_20
ARPOTweety21	652130.814	3765656.149	ARPO_21
ARPOTweety22	652696.499	3765656.149	ARPO_22
ARPOTweety23	652555.078	3765514.728	ARPO_23
ARPOTweety24	652413.656	3765373.306	ARPO_24
ARPOTweety25	652555.078	3765231.885	ARPO_25
ARPOTweety26	652837.920	3764949.042	ARPO_26
ARPOTweety27	652979.342	3764807.621	ARPO_27
ARPOTweety28	659908.988	3761837.773	ARPO_28
ARPOTweety29	660191.831	3761837.773	ARPO_29
ARPOTweety30	660474.674	3761837.773	ARPO_30
ARPOTweety31	660050.410	3761696.351	ARPO_31
ARPOTweety32	660616.095	3761696.351	ARPO_32
ARPOTweety33	659908.988	3761554.930	ARPO_33
ARPOTweety34	660191.831	3761554.930	ARPO_34
ARPOTweety35	660333.252	3761413.508	ARPO_35
ARPOTweety36	660898.938	3761413.508	ARPO_36

Table B.2: Waypoints for Effigy Mounds National Monument, Iowa – UTM Zone 15 North, Datum 1983 (Conus).

Plot I.D	X Coordinate (Easting)	Y Coordinate (Northing)	Inventory I.D Number
EFMOTweety1	647837.313	4774424.000	EFMO_1
EFMOTweety2	647783.375	4774027.500	EFMO_2
EFMOTweety3	647729.438	4773631.000	EFMO_3
EFMOTweety4	645297.438	4773558.500	EFMO_4
EFMOTweety5	645693.813	4773504.500	EFMO_5
EFMOTweety6	646090.125	4773450.500	EFMO_6
EFMOTweety7	646486.500	4773396.500	EFMO_7
EFMOTweety8	647675.563	4773235.000	EFMO_8
EFMOTweety9	648071.875	4773181.000	EFMO_9
EFMOTweety10	644847.188	4773216.000	EFMO_10
EFMOTweety11	645243.563	4773162.000	EFMO_11
EFMOTweety12	645639.875	4773108.000	EFMO_12
EFMOTweety13	646036.250	4773054.000	EFMO_13
EFMOTweety14	646432.563	4773000.000	EFMO_14
EFMOTweety15	647225.313	4772892.500	EFMO_15
EFMOTweety16	647621.625	4772838.500	EFMO_16
EFMOTweety17	648018.000	4772784.500	EFMO_17
EFMOTweety18	644793.250	4772819.500	EFMO_18
EFMOTweety19	645189.625	4772765.500	EFMO_19
EFMOTweety20	645586.000	4772711.500	EFMO_20
EFMOTweety21	645982.313	4772658.000	EFMO_21
EFMOTweety22	646378.688	4772604.000	EFMO_22
EFMOTweety23	646775.063	4772550.000	EFMO_23
EFMOTweety24	647171.375	4772496.000	EFMO_24
EFMOTweety25	647567.750	4772442.000	EFMO_25
EFMOTweety26	643946.688	4772531.000	EFMO_26
EFMOTweety27	645532.063	4772315.500	EFMO_27
EFMOTweety28	645928.438	4772261.500	EFMO_28
EFMOTweety29	646324.750	4772207.500	EFMO_29
EFMOTweety30	646721.125	4772153.500	EFMO_30
EFMOTweety31	647117.500	4772099.500	EFMO_31
EFMOTweety32	647513.813	4772046.000	EFMO_32
EFMOTweety33	643892.750	4772134.500	EFMO_33
EFMOTweety34	645874.500	4771865.000	EFMO_34
EFMOTweety35	646667.188	4771757.000	EFMO_35
EFMOTweety36	647063.563	4771703.500	EFMO_36
EFMOTweety37	647459.938	4771649.500	EFMO_37
EFMOTweety38	647856.250	4771595.500	EFMO_38
EFMOTweety39	645424.250	4771522.500	EFMO_39
EFMOTweety40	645820.625	4771468.500	EFMO_40
EFMOTweety41	646613.313	4771361.000	EFMO_41
EFMOTweety42	647406.000	4771253.000	EFMO_42
EFMOTweety43	647802.375	4771199.000	EFMO_43
EFMOTweety44	647352.063	4770856.500	EFMO_44
EFMOTweety45	647748.438	4770803.000	EFMO_45
EFMOTweety46	647298.188	4770460.500	EFMO_46
EFMOTweety47	647694.563	4770406.500	EFMO_47
EFMOTweety48	647640.625	4770010.000	EFMO_48
EFMOTweety49	648037.000	4769956.000	EFMO_49
EFMOTweety50	649428.607	4756445.473	EFMO_50
EFMOTweety51	649374.693	4756049.123	EFMO_51
EFMOTweety52	649320.780	4755652.773	EFMO_52

Table B.3: Waypoints for George Washington Carver National Monument, Missouri – UTM Zone 15 North, Datum 1983 (Conus).

Plot I.D.	X Coordinate (Easting)	Y Coordinate (Northing)	Inventory I.D. Number
GWCATweety1	379070.421	4094759.924	GWCA_1
GWCATweety2	379211.842	4094759.924	GWCA_2
GWCATweety3	379353.263	4094759.924	GWCA_3
GWCATweety4	379494.685	4094759.924	GWCA_4
GWCATweety5	379636.106	4094759.924	GWCA_5
GWCATweety6	379141.131	4094689.214	GWCA_6
GWCATweety7	379282.553	4094689.214	GWCA_7
GWCATweety8	379423.974	4094689.214	GWCA_8
GWCATweety9	379565.395	4094689.214	GWCA_9
GWCATweety10	379706.817	4094689.214	GWCA_10
GWCATweety11	379070.421	4094618.503	GWCA_11
GWCATweety12	379211.842	4094618.503	GWCA_12
GWCATweety13	379353.263	4094618.503	GWCA_13
GWCATweety14	379494.685	4094618.503	GWCA_14
GWCATweety15	379636.106	4094618.503	GWCA_15
GWCATweety16	379141.131	4094547.792	GWCA_16
GWCATweety17	379282.553	4094547.792	GWCA_17
GWCATweety18	379423.974	4094547.792	GWCA_18
GWCATweety19	379565.395	4094547.792	GWCA_19
GWCATweety20	379706.817	4094547.792	GWCA_20
GWCATweety21	379070.421	4094477.082	GWCA_21
GWCATweety22	379211.842	4094477.082	GWCA_22
GWCATweety23	379353.263	4094477.082	GWCA_23
GWCATweety24	379494.685	4094477.082	GWCA_24
GWCATweety25	379636.106	4094477.082	GWCA_25
GWCATweety26	379141.131	4094406.371	GWCA_26
GWCATweety27	379282.553	4094406.371	GWCA_27
GWCATweety28	379423.974	4094406.371	GWCA_28
GWCATweety29	379565.395	4094406.371	GWCA_29
GWCATweety30	379706.817	4094406.371	GWCA_30
GWCATweety31	379070.421	4094335.660	GWCA_31
GWCATweety32	379211.842	4094335.660	GWCA_32
GWCATweety33	379353.263	4094335.660	GWCA_33
GWCATweety34	379494.685	4094335.660	GWCA_34
GWCATweety35	379636.106	4094335.660	GWCA_35
GWCATweety36	379141.131	4094264.949	GWCA_36
GWCATweety37	379282.553	4094264.949	GWCA_37
GWCATweety38	379423.974	4094264.949	GWCA_38
GWCATweety39	379565.395	4094264.949	GWCA_39
GWCATweety40	379706.817	4094264.949	GWCA_40
GWCATweety41	379070.421	4094194.239	GWCA_41
GWCATweety42	379211.842	4094194.239	GWCA_42
GWCATweety43	379141.131	4094123.528	GWCA_43
GWCATweety44	379282.553	4094123.528	GWCA_44
GWCATweety45	379565.395	4094123.528	GWCA_45
GWCATweety46	379070.421	4094052.817	GWCA_46
GWCATweety47	379353.263	4094052.817	GWCA_47
GWCATweety48	379636.106	4094052.817	GWCA_48
GWCATweety49	379141.131	4093982.107	GWCA_49
GWCATweety50	379282.553	4093982.107	GWCA_50
GWCATweety51	379423.974	4093982.107	GWCA_51
GWCATweety52	379565.395	4093982.107	GWCA_52

Table B.3: continued

Plot I.D.	X Coordinate (Easting)	Y Coordinate (Northing)	Inventory I.D. Number
GWCATweety53	379070.421	4093911.396	GWCA_53
GWCATweety54	379211.842	4093911.396	GWCA_54
GWCATweety55	379353.263	4093911.396	GWCA_55
GWCATweety56	379494.685	4093911.396	GWCA_56
GWCATweety57	379636.106	4093911.396	GWCA_57
GWCATweety58	379141.131	4093840.685	GWCA_58
GWCATweety59	379282.553	4093840.685	GWCA_59
GWCATweety60	379423.974	4093840.685	GWCA_60
GWCATweety61	379565.395	4093840.685	GWCA_61
GWCATweety62	379070.421	4093769.975	GWCA_62
GWCATweety63	379211.842	4093769.975	GWCA_63
GWCATweety64	379353.263	4093769.975	GWCA_64
GWCATweety65	379494.685	4093769.975	GWCA_65
GWCATweety66	379636.106	4093769.975	GWCA_66
GWCATweety67	379141.131	4093699.264	GWCA_67
GWCATweety68	379282.553	4093699.264	GWCA_68
GWCATweety69	379423.974	4093699.264	GWCA_69
GWCATweety70	379565.395	4093699.264	GWCA_70

Table B.4: Waypoints for Herbert Hoover National Historic Site, Iowa – UTM Zone 15 North, Datum 1983 (Conus).

Plot I.D.	X Coordinate (Easting)	Y Coordinate (Northing)	Inventory I.D. Number
HEHOTweety1	636971.393	4614410.700	HEHO_1
HEHOTweety2	637005.863	4614129.966	HEHO_2
HEHOTweety3	636882.731	4613972.364	HEHO_3
HEHOTweety4	637286.597	4614164.436	HEHO_4
HEHOTweety5	637163.465	4614006.834	HEHO_5
HEHOTweety6	637040.333	4613849.232	HEHO_6
HEHOTweety7	637567.332	4614198.906	HEHO_7
HEHOTweety8	637444.200	4614041.303	HEHO_8
HEHOTweety9	637321.067	4613883.701	HEHO_9
HEHOTweety10	637050.194	4614349.134	HEHO_10
HEHOTweety11	636988.628	4614270.333	HEHO_11
HEHOTweety12	636927.062	4614191.532	HEHO_12
HEHOTweety13	637067.429	4614208.767	HEHO_13
HEHOTweety14	636944.297	4614051.165	HEHO_14
HEHOTweety15	637146.230	4614147.201	HEHO_15
HEHOTweety16	637084.664	4614068.400	HEHO_16
HEHOTweety17	637023.098	4613989.599	HEHO_17
HEHOTweety18	636961.532	4613910.798	HEHO_18
HEHOTweety19	637225.031	4614085.635	HEHO_19
HEHOTweety20	637101.899	4613928.033	HEHO_20
HEHOTweety21	637426.965	4614181.671	HEHO_21
HEHOTweety22	637365.399	4614102.870	HEHO_22
HEHOTweety23	637303.832	4614024.069	HEHO_23
HEHOTweety24	637242.266	4613945.268	HEHO_24
HEHOTweety25	637505.766	4614120.105	HEHO_25
HEHOTweety26	637382.633	4613962.502	HEHO_26
HEHOTweety27	636892.592	4614472.267	HEHO_27
HEHOTweety28	636909.827	4614331.899	HEHO_28
HEHOTweety29	637111.760	4614427.935	HEHO_29
HEHOTweety30	637190.561	4614366.369	HEHO_30
HEHOTweety31	637128.995	4614287.568	HEHO_31
HEHOTweety32	637330.929	4614383.604	HEHO_32
HEHOTweety33	637269.363	4614304.803	HEHO_33
HEHOTweety34	637471.296	4614400.839	HEHO_34
HEHOTweety35	637409.730	4614322.038	HEHO_35
HEHOTweety36	637348.164	4614243.237	HEHO_36
HEHOTweety37	637611.663	4614418.074	HEHO_37
HEHOTweety38	637488.531	4614260.472	HEHO_38

Table B.5: Waypoints for Homestead National Monument of America, Nebraska – UTM Zone 14 North, Datum 1983 (Conus).

Plot I.D.	X Coordinate (Easting)	Y Coordinate (Northing)	Inventory I.D. Number
HOMETweety1	684124.165	4462295.543	HOME_1
HOMETweety2	684194.876	4462224.832	HOME_2
HOMETweety3	684124.165	4462154.122	HOME_3
HOMETweety4	684053.455	4462083.411	HOME_4
HOMETweety5	684194.876	4462083.411	HOME_5
HOMETweety6	684124.165	4462012.701	HOME_6
HOMETweety7	684194.876	4461941.990	HOME_7
HOMETweety8	684336.297	4461941.990	HOME_8
HOMETweety9	684477.719	4461941.990	HOME_9
HOMETweety10	684619.140	4461941.990	HOME_10
HOMETweety11	684124.165	4461871.279	HOME_11
HOMETweety12	684265.587	4461871.279	HOME_12
HOMETweety13	684407.008	4461871.279	HOME_13
HOMETweety14	684548.430	4461871.279	HOME_14
HOMETweety15	684053.455	4461800.568	HOME_15
HOMETweety16	684194.876	4461800.568	HOME_16
HOMETweety17	684336.297	4461800.568	HOME_17
HOMETweety18	684477.719	4461800.568	HOME_18
HOMETweety19	684619.140	4461800.568	HOME_19
HOMETweety20	683841.323	4461729.858	HOME_20
HOMETweety21	683982.744	4461729.858	HOME_21
HOMETweety22	684124.165	4461729.858	HOME_22
HOMETweety23	684265.587	4461729.858	HOME_23
HOMETweety24	684407.008	4461729.858	HOME_24
HOMETweety25	684548.429	4461729.858	HOME_25
HOMETweety26	684689.851	4461729.858	HOME_26
HOMETweety27	683770.612	4461659.147	HOME_27
HOMETweety28	683912.033	4461659.147	HOME_28
HOMETweety29	684053.455	4461659.147	HOME_29
HOMETweety30	684194.876	4461659.147	HOME_30
HOMETweety31	684194.876	4462366.254	HOME_31
HOMETweety32	684053.455	4462224.832	HOME_32
HOMETweety33	683982.744	4462154.122	HOME_33
HOMETweety34	683982.744	4462012.700	HOME_34
HOMETweety35	683629.191	4461941.990	HOME_35
HOMETweety36	683770.612	4461941.990	HOME_36
HOMETweety37	683912.033	4461941.990	HOME_37
HOMETweety38	684053.455	4461941.990	HOME_38
HOMETweety39	683558.480	4461871.279	HOME_39
HOMETweety40	683699.901	4461871.279	HOME_40
HOMETweety41	683841.323	4461871.279	HOME_41
HOMETweety42	683982.744	4461871.279	HOME_42
HOMETweety43	683629.191	4461800.568	HOME_43
HOMETweety44	683770.612	4461800.568	HOME_44
HOMETweety45	683912.033	4461800.568	HOME_45
HOMETweety46	683558.480	4461729.858	HOME_46
HOMETweety47	683699.901	4461729.858	HOME_47
HOMETweety48	683629.191	4461659.147	HOME_48

Table B.6: Waypoints for Hopewell Cultural National Historical Park, Ohio – UTM Zone 17 North, Datum 1983 (Conus).

Plot I.D.	X Coordinate (Easting)	Y Coordinate (Northing)	Inventory I.D. Number
HOCUTweety1	327116.650	4360162.840	MCVCP1
HOCUTweety2	327116.650	4360562.010	MCVCP2
HOCUTweety3	327116.650	4360953.620	MCVCP4
HOCUTweety4	327503.720	4360562.010	MCVCP3
HOCUTweety5	329876.420	4360965.010	HTVCP1
HOCUTweety6	329534.060	4360965.010	HTVCP2
HOCUTweety7	329135.980	4360965.010	HTVCP3
HOCUTweety8	329135.980	4361364.530	HTVCP5
HOCUTweety9	329534.060	4361364.530	HTVCP6
HOCUTweety10	329534.060	4361765.480	HTVCP7
HOCUTweety11	329648.180	4360790.860	HTVCP8
HOCUTweety12	319135.000	4358980.000	HWVCP1
HOCUTweety13	319534.000	4359380.000	HWVCP2
HOCUTweety14	319534.000	4358980.000	HWVCP3
HOCUTweety15	319625.000	4358670.000	HWVCP4
HOCUTweety16	319933.000	4358980.000	HWVCP5
HOCUTweety17	319933.000	4359380.000	HWVCP6
HOCUTweety18	320332.000	4358980.000	HWVCP7
HOCUTweety19	334310.530	4350593.650	HBVCP1
HOCUTweety20	334364.530	4351727.860	HBVCP3
HOCUTweety21	334310.530	4352141.990	HBVCP4
HOCUTweety22	334693.860	4351727.860	HBVCP5
HOCUTweety23	334693.860	4351337.690	HBVCP6
HOCUTweety24	308213.000	4345591.000	SPVCP1
HOCUTweety25	308213.000	4345192.000	SPVCP2
HOCUTweety26	308213.000	4344810.000	SPVCP3
HOCUTweety27	308802.000	4345059.999	SPVCP4

Table B.7: Waypoints for Lincoln Boyhood National Memorial, Indiana – UTM Zone 16 North, Datum 1983 (Conus).

Plot I.D.	X Coordinate (Easting)	Y Coordinate (Northing)	Inventory I.D. Number
LIBOTweety1	500432.278	4219695.381	LIBO_1
LIBOTweety2	500220.146	4219624.671	LIBO_2
LIBOTweety3	500432.278	4219553.960	LIBO_3
LIBOTweety4	500361.567	4219483.249	LIBO_4
LIBOTweety5	500432.278	4219412.539	LIBO_5
LIBOTweety6	500361.567	4219341.828	LIBO_6
LIBOTweety7	500290.856	4219271.117	LIBO_7
LIBOTweety8	500432.278	4219271.117	LIBO_8
LIBOTweety9	500361.567	4219200.407	LIBO_9
LIBOTweety10	500432.278	4219129.696	LIBO_10
LIBOTweety11	Not Sampled		LIBO_11
LIBOTweety12	Not Sampled		LIBO_12
LIBOTweety13	500290.856	4218988.274	LIBO_13
LIBOTweety14	500432.278	4218988.274	LIBO_14
LIBOTweety15	Not Sampled		LIBO_15
LIBOTweety16	500361.567	4218917.564	LIBO_16
LIBOTweety17	500502.988	4218917.564	LIBO_17
LIBOTweety18	Not Sampled		LIBO_18
LIBOTweety19	500290.856	4218846.853	LIBO_19
LIBOTweety20	500432.278	4218846.853	LIBO_20
LIBOTweety21	Not Sampled		LIBO_21
LIBOTweety22	500220.146	4218776.142	LIBO_22
LIBOTweety23	500361.567	4218776.142	LIBO_23
LIBOTweety24	500502.988	4218776.142	LIBO_24
LIBOTweety25	Not Sampled		LIBO_25
LIBOTweety26	500149.435	4218705.432	LIBO_26
LIBOTweety27	500290.856	4218705.432	LIBO_27
LIBOTweety28	500432.278	4218705.432	LIBO_28
LIBOTweety29	500078.724	4218634.721	LIBO_29
LIBOTweety30	500220.146	4218634.721	LIBO_30
LIBOTweety31	500502.988	4218634.721	LIBO_31
LIBOTweety32	500008.014	4218564.010	LIBO_32
LIBOTweety33	500149.435	4218564.010	LIBO_33
LIBOTweety34	500290.856	4218564.010	LIBO_34
LIBOTweety35	500432.278	4218564.010	LIBO_35
LIBOTweety36	499937.303	4218493.300	LIBO_36
LIBOTweety37	500078.724	4218493.300	LIBO_37
LIBOTweety38	500220.146	4218493.300	LIBO_38
LIBOTweety39	500502.988	4218493.300	LIBO_39
LIBOTweety40	500220.146	4218351.878	LIBO_40
LIBOTweety41	500502.988	4218351.878	LIBO_41

Table B.8: Waypoints for Pea Ridge National Military Park, Arkansas – UTM Zone 15 North, Datum 1983 (Conus).

Plot I.D.	X Coordinate (Easting)	Y Coordinate (Northing)	Inventory I.D. Number
PERITweety1	405072.520	4036536.798	PERI_1
PERITweety2	405638.205	4036536.798	PERI_2
PERITweety3	406203.891	4036536.798	PERI_3
PERITweety4	407335.262	4036536.798	PERI_4
PERITweety5	404789.677	4036253.955	PERI_5
PERITweety6	405355.363	4036253.955	PERI_6
PERITweety7	405921.048	4036253.955	PERI_7
PERITweety8	406486.733	4036253.955	PERI_8
PERITweety9	407052.419	4036253.955	PERI_9
PERITweety10	407618.104	4036253.955	PERI_10
PERITweety11	408183.790	4036253.955	PERI_11
PERITweety12	409315.161	4036253.955	PERI_12
PERITweety13	409880.846	4036253.955	PERI_13
PERITweety14	405072.520	4035971.112	PERI_14
PERITweety15	405638.205	4035971.112	PERI_15
PERITweety16	406203.891	4035971.112	PERI_16
PERITweety17	406769.576	4035971.112	PERI_17
PERITweety18	407335.262	4035971.112	PERI_18
PERITweety19	407900.947	4035971.112	PERI_19
PERITweety20	409598.003	4035971.112	PERI_20
PERITweety21	405355.363	4035688.269	PERI_21
PERITweety22	405921.048	4035688.269	PERI_22
PERITweety23	406486.733	4035688.269	PERI_23
PERITweety24	407052.419	4035688.269	PERI_24
PERITweety25	407618.104	4035688.269	PERI_25
PERITweety26	408183.790	4035688.269	PERI_26
PERITweety27	408749.475	4035688.269	PERI_27
PERITweety28	409315.161	4035688.269	PERI_28
PERITweety29	409880.846	4035688.269	PERI_29
PERITweety30	405072.520	4035405.427	PERI_30
PERITweety31	405638.205	4035405.427	PERI_31
PERITweety32	406203.891	4035405.427	PERI_32
PERITweety33	406769.576	4035405.427	PERI_33
PERITweety34	407335.262	4035405.427	PERI_34
PERITweety35	407900.947	4035405.427	PERI_35
PERITweety36	408466.632	4035405.427	PERI_36
PERITweety37	409032.318	4035405.427	PERI_37
PERITweety38	409598.003	4035405.427	PERI_38
PERITweety39	410163.689	4035405.427	PERI_39
PERITweety40	405355.363	4035122.584	PERI_40
PERITweety41	405921.048	4035122.584	PERI_41
PERITweety42	406486.733	4035122.584	PERI_42
PERITweety43	407052.419	4035122.584	PERI_43
PERITweety44	407618.104	4035122.584	PERI_44
PERITweety45	408183.790	4035122.584	PERI_45
PERITweety46	408749.475	4035122.584	PERI_46
PERITweety47	409315.161	4035122.584	PERI_47
PERITweety48	409880.846	4035122.584	PERI_48
PERITweety49	405072.520	4034839.741	PERI_49
PERITweety50	405638.205	4034839.741	PERI_50
PERITweety51	406203.891	4034839.741	PERI_51
PERITweety52	406769.576	4034839.741	PERI_52

Table B.8: continued

Plot I.D.	X Coordinate (Easting)	Y Coordinate (Northing)	Inventory I.D. Number
PERITweety53	407335.262	4034839.741	PERI_53
PERITweety54	407900.947	4034839.741	PERI_54
PERITweety55	408466.632	4034839.741	PERI_55
PERITweety56	409032.318	4034839.741	PERI_56
PERITweety57	409598.003	4034839.741	PERI_57
PERITweety58	410163.689	4034839.741	PERI_58
PERITweety59	405355.363	4034556.899	PERI_59
PERITweety60	405921.048	4034556.899	PERI_60
PERITweety61	406486.733	4034556.899	PERI_61
PERITweety62	407052.419	4034556.899	PERI_62
PERITweety63	407618.104	4034556.899	PERI_63
PERITweety64	408183.790	4034556.899	PERI_64
PERITweety65	408749.475	4034556.899	PERI_65
PERITweety66	409315.161	4034556.899	PERI_66
PERITweety67	409880.846	4034556.899	PERI_67
PERITweety68	405072.520	4034274.056	PERI_68
PERITweety69	405638.205	4034274.056	PERI_69
PERITweety70	406203.891	4034274.056	PERI_70
PERITweety71	406769.576	4034274.056	PERI_71
PERITweety72	407335.262	4034274.056	PERI_72
PERITweety73	407900.947	4034274.056	PERI_73
PERITweety74	408466.632	4034274.056	PERI_74
PERITweety75	409032.318	4034274.056	PERI_75
PERITweety76	409598.003	4034274.056	PERI_76
PERITweety77	410163.689	4034274.056	PERI_77
PERITweety78	404789.677	4033991.213	PERI_78
PERITweety79	405355.363	4033991.213	PERI_79
PERITweety80	405921.048	4033991.213	PERI_80
PERITweety81	406486.733	4033991.213	PERI_81
PERITweety82	407052.419	4033991.213	PERI_82
PERITweety83	407618.104	4033991.213	PERI_83
PERITweety84	408183.790	4033991.213	PERI_84
PERITweety85	408749.475	4033991.213	PERI_85
PERITweety86	405072.520	4033708.370	PERI_86
PERITweety87	405638.205	4033708.370	PERI_87
PERITweety88	406203.891	4033708.370	PERI_88
PERITweety89	406769.576	4033708.370	PERI_89
PERITweety90	407335.262	4033708.370	PERI_90
PERITweety91	407900.947	4033708.370	PERI_91
PERITweety92	405355.363	4033425.528	PERI_92
PERITweety93	405921.048	4033425.528	PERI_93
PERITweety94	406486.733	4033425.528	PERI_94
PERITweety95	407052.419	4033425.528	PERI_95
PERITweety96	405638.205	4033142.685	PERI_96
PERITweety97	405355.363	4032859.842	PERI_97
PERITweety98	405638.205	4031445.629	PERI_98
PERITweety99	405355.363	4031162.786	PERI_99

Table B.9: Waypoints for Pipestone National Monument, Minnesota – UTM Zone 14 North, Datum 1983 (Conus).

Plot I.D.	X Coordinate (Easting)	Y Coordinate (Northing)	Inventory I.D. Number
PIPETweety1	714523.683	4877379.195	PIPE_1
PIPETweety2	714665.105	4877379.195	PIPE_2
PIPETweety3	714311.551	4877308.484	PIPE_3
PIPETweety4	714452.973	4877308.484	PIPE_4
PIPETweety5	714594.394	4877308.484	PIPE_5
PIPETweety6	714735.815	4877308.484	PIPE_6
PIPETweety7	714382.262	4877237.774	PIPE_7
PIPETweety8	714523.683	4877237.774	PIPE_8
PIPETweety9	714665.105	4877237.774	PIPE_9
PIPETweety10	714028.708	4877167.063	PIPE_10
PIPETweety11	714170.130	4877167.063	PIPE_11
PIPETweety12	714311.551	4877167.063	PIPE_12
PIPETweety13	714452.973	4877167.063	PIPE_13
PIPETweety14	714594.394	4877167.063	PIPE_14
PIPETweety15	714735.815	4877167.063	PIPE_15
PIPETweety16	713957.998	4877096.352	PIPE_16
PIPETweety17	714099.419	4877096.352	PIPE_17
PIPETweety18	714240.841	4877096.352	PIPE_18
PIPETweety19	714382.262	4877096.352	PIPE_19
PIPETweety20	714523.683	4877096.352	PIPE_20
PIPETweety21	714665.105	4877096.352	PIPE_21
PIPETweety22	714806.526	4877096.352	PIPE_22
PIPETweety23	714028.708	4877025.642	PIPE_23
PIPETweety24	714170.130	4877025.642	PIPE_24
PIPETweety25	714311.551	4877025.642	PIPE_25
PIPETweety26	714452.973	4877025.642	PIPE_26
PIPETweety27	714594.394	4877025.642	PIPE_27
PIPETweety28	714735.815	4877025.642	PIPE_28
PIPETweety29	714877.237	4877025.642	PIPE_29
PIPETweety30	713957.998	4876954.931	PIPE_30
PIPETweety31	714099.419	4876954.931	PIPE_31
PIPETweety32	714240.841	4876954.931	PIPE_32
PIPETweety33	714382.262	4876954.931	PIPE_33
PIPETweety34	714665.105	4876954.931	PIPE_34
PIPETweety35	714806.526	4876954.931	PIPE_35
PIPETweety36	714028.708	4876884.220	PIPE_36
PIPETweety37	714170.130	4876884.220	PIPE_37
PIPETweety38	714311.551	4876884.220	PIPE_38
PIPETweety39	714594.394	4876884.220	PIPE_39
PIPETweety40	714735.815	4876884.220	PIPE_40
PIPETweety41	714877.237	4876884.220	PIPE_41
PIPETweety42	714099.419	4876813.510	PIPE_42
PIPETweety43	714240.841	4876813.510	PIPE_43
PIPETweety44	714523.683	4876813.510	PIPE_44
PIPETweety45	714806.526	4876813.510	PIPE_45
PIPETweety46	714947.947	4876813.510	PIPE_46
PIPETweety47	714028.708	4876742.799	PIPE_47
PIPETweety48	714170.130	4876742.799	PIPE_48
PIPETweety49	714452.973	4876742.799	PIPE_49
PIPETweety50	714877.237	4876742.799	PIPE_50
PIPETweety51	714099.419	4876672.088	PIPE_51
PIPETweety52	714240.841	4876672.088	PIPE_52

Table B.9: continued

Plot I.D.	X Coordinate (Easting)	Y Coordinate (Northing)	Inventory I.D. Number
PIPETweety53	714382.262	4876672.088	PIPE_53
PIPETweety54	714947.947	4876672.088	PIPE_54
PIPETweety55	714028.708	4876601.378	PIPE_55
PIPETweety56	714170.130	4876601.378	PIPE_56
PIPETweety57	714311.551	4876601.378	PIPE_57
PIPETweety58	714452.973	4876601.378	PIPE_58
PIPETweety59	714877.237	4876601.378	PIPE_59
PIPETweety60	714099.419	4876530.667	PIPE_60
PIPETweety61	714240.841	4876530.667	PIPE_61
PIPETweety62	714382.262	4876530.667	PIPE_62
PIPETweety63	714947.947	4876530.667	PIPE_63
PIPETweety64	714028.708	4876459.956	PIPE_64
PIPETweety65	714170.130	4876459.956	PIPE_65
PIPETweety66	714877.237	4876459.956	PIPE_66
PIPETweety67	714099.419	4876389.245	PIPE_67
PIPETweety68	714240.841	4876389.245	PIPE_68

Table B.10: Waypoints for Tallgrass Prairie National Preserve, Kansas – UTM Zone 14 North, Datum 1983 (Conus).

Plot I.D.	X Coordinate (Easting)	Y Coordinate (Northing)	Inventory I.D. Number
TAPRTweety1	711444.688	4263461.000	TAPR_1
TAPRTweety2	710113.438	4262906.000	TAPR_2
TAPRTweety3	711555.625	4262906.000	TAPR_3
TAPRTweety4	711000.938	4262795.500	TAPR_4
TAPRTweety5	710446.250	4262684.500	TAPR_5
TAPRTweety6	711888.438	4262684.500	TAPR_6
TAPRTweety7	709891.563	4262573.500	TAPR_7
TAPRTweety8	711333.750	4262573.500	TAPR_8
TAPRTweety9	710779.063	4262462.500	TAPR_9
TAPRTweety10	710224.375	4262351.500	TAPR_10
TAPRTweety11	711666.563	4262351.500	TAPR_11
TAPRTweety12	711111.875	4262240.500	TAPR_12
TAPRTweety13	710557.188	4262129.500	TAPR_13
TAPRTweety14	711999.375	4262129.500	TAPR_14
TAPRTweety15	710002.500	4262018.500	TAPR_15
TAPRTweety16	711444.688	4262018.500	TAPR_16
TAPRTweety17	710890.000	4261907.500	TAPR_17
TAPRTweety18	710335.313	4261797.000	TAPR_18
TAPRTweety19	711777.500	4261797.000	TAPR_19
TAPRTweety20	709780.563	4261686.000	TAPR_20
TAPRTweety21	711222.813	4261686.000	TAPR_21
TAPRTweety22	710668.125	4261575.000	TAPR_22
TAPRTweety23	711555.625	4261464.000	TAPR_23
TAPRTweety24	709891.563	4261131.000	TAPR_24
TAPRTweety25	710779.063	4261020.000	TAPR_25
TAPRTweety26	710224.375	4260909.500	TAPR_26
TAPRTweety27	711666.563	4260909.500	TAPR_27
TAPRTweety28	711111.875	4260798.500	TAPR_28
TAPRTweety29	710557.188	4260687.500	TAPR_29
TAPRTweety30	711999.375	4260687.500	TAPR_30
TAPRTweety31	710002.500	4260576.500	TAPR_31
TAPRTweety32	711444.688	4260576.500	TAPR_32
TAPRTweety33	710890.000	4260465.500	TAPR_33
TAPRTweety34	710335.313	4260354.500	TAPR_34
TAPRTweety35	711777.500	4260354.500	TAPR_35
TAPRTweety36	711222.813	4260243.500	TAPR_36
TAPRTweety37	710668.125	4260132.500	TAPR_37
TAPRTweety38	710113.438	4260022.000	TAPR_38
TAPRTweety39	711555.625	4260022.000	TAPR_39
TAPRTweety40	711000.938	4259911.000	TAPR_40
TAPRTweety41	710446.250	4259800.000	TAPR_41
TAPRTweety42	711888.438	4259800.000	TAPR_42
TAPRTweety43	709891.563	4259689.000	TAPR_43
TAPRTweety44	711333.750	4259689.000	TAPR_44
TAPRTweety45	712776.000	4259689.000	TAPR_45
TAPRTweety46	710779.063	4259578.000	TAPR_46
TAPRTweety47	712221.250	4259578.000	TAPR_47
TAPRTweety48	710224.375	4259467.000	TAPR_48
TAPRTweety49	711666.563	4259467.000	TAPR_49
TAPRTweety50	711111.875	4259356.000	TAPR_50
TAPRTweety51	712554.063	4259356.000	TAPR_51
TAPRTweety52	710557.188	4259245.000	TAPR_52

Table B.10: continued

Plot I.D.	X Coordinate (Easting)	Y Coordinate (Northing)	Inventory I.D. Number
TAPRTweety53	711999.375	4259245.000	TAPR_53
TAPRTweety54	710002.500	4259134.000	TAPR_54
TAPRTweety55	711444.688	4259134.000	TAPR_55
TAPRTweety56	712886.938	4259134.000	TAPR_56
TAPRTweety57	710890.000	4259023.500	TAPR_57
TAPRTweety58	712332.188	4259023.500	TAPR_58
TAPRTweety59	710335.313	4258912.500	TAPR_59
TAPRTweety60	711777.500	4258912.500	TAPR_60
TAPRTweety61	711222.813	4258801.500	TAPR_61
TAPRTweety62	712665.063	4258801.500	TAPR_62
TAPRTweety63	710668.125	4258690.500	TAPR_63
TAPRTweety64	712110.313	4258690.500	TAPR_64
TAPRTweety65	711333.750	4258246.500	TAPR_65
TAPRTweety66	712776.000	4258246.500	TAPR_66
TAPRTweety67	710779.063	4258136.000	TAPR_67
TAPRTweety68	710224.375	4258025.000	TAPR_68
TAPRTweety69	711666.563	4258025.000	TAPR_69
TAPRTweety70	711111.875	4257914.000	TAPR_70
TAPRTweety71	710557.188	4257803.000	TAPR_71
TAPRTweety72	711999.375	4257803.000	TAPR_72
TAPRTweety73	710002.500	4257692.000	TAPR_73
TAPRTweety74	711444.688	4257692.000	TAPR_74
TAPRTweety75	712886.938	4257692.000	TAPR_75
TAPRTweety76	710890.000	4257581.000	TAPR_76
TAPRTweety77	710335.313	4257470.000	TAPR_77
TAPRTweety78	711777.500	4257470.000	TAPR_78
TAPRTweety79	711222.813	4257359.000	TAPR_79
TAPRTweety80	710668.125	4257248.500	TAPR_80
TAPRTweety81	712110.313	4257248.500	TAPR_81
TAPRTweety82	710113.438	4257137.500	TAPR_82
TAPRTweety83	711555.625	4257137.500	TAPR_83
TAPRTweety84	714218.188	4256804.500	TAPR_84
TAPRTweety85	713663.500	4256693.500	TAPR_85
TAPRTweety86	710224.375	4256582.500	TAPR_86
TAPRTweety87	711666.563	4256582.500	TAPR_87
TAPRTweety88	714551.000	4256582.500	TAPR_88
TAPRTweety89	711111.875	4256471.500	TAPR_89
TAPRTweety90	710557.188	4256360.500	TAPR_90
TAPRTweety91	711999.375	4256360.500	TAPR_91
TAPRTweety92	710002.500	4256250.000	TAPR_92
TAPRTweety93	711444.688	4256250.000	TAPR_93
TAPRTweety94	714329.125	4256250.000	TAPR_94
TAPRTweety95	710890.000	4256139.000	TAPR_95
TAPRTweety96	712332.188	4256139.000	TAPR_96
TAPRTweety97	710335.313	4256028.000	TAPR_97
TAPRTweety98	711777.500	4256028.000	TAPR_98
TAPRTweety99	711222.813	4255917.000	TAPR_99
TAPRTweety100	710668.125	4255806.000	TAPR_100
TAPRTweety101	712110.313	4255806.000	TAPR_101
TAPRTweety102	713552.563	4255806.000	TAPR_102
TAPRTweety103	710113.438	4255695.000	TAPR_103
TAPRTweety104	711555.625	4255695.000	TAPR_104
TAPRTweety105	714440.063	4255695.000	TAPR_105

Table B.10: continued

Plot I.D.	X Coordinate (Easting)	Y Coordinate (Northing)	Inventory I.D. Number
TAPRTweety106	711000.938	4255584.000	TAPR_106
TAPRTweety107	712443.125	4255584.000	TAPR_107
TAPRTweety108	710446.250	4255473.000	TAPR_108
TAPRTweety109	711888.438	4255473.000	TAPR_109
TAPRTweety110	713663.500	4255251.500	TAPR_110
TAPRTweety111	714551.000	4255140.500	TAPR_111
TAPRTweety112	715993.250	4255140.500	TAPR_112
TAPRTweety113	717435.438	4255140.500	TAPR_113
TAPRTweety114	711111.875	4255029.500	TAPR_114
TAPRTweety115	712554.063	4255029.500	TAPR_115
TAPRTweety116	715438.563	4255029.500	TAPR_116
TAPRTweety117	716880.750	4255029.500	TAPR_117
TAPRTweety118	710557.188	4254918.500	TAPR_118
TAPRTweety119	711999.375	4254918.500	TAPR_119
TAPRTweety120	716326.063	4254918.500	TAPR_120
TAPRTweety121	717768.250	4254918.500	TAPR_121
TAPRTweety122	710002.500	4254807.500	TAPR_122
TAPRTweety123	711444.688	4254807.500	TAPR_123
TAPRTweety124	712886.938	4254807.500	TAPR_124
TAPRTweety125	714329.125	4254807.500	TAPR_125
TAPRTweety126	715771.375	4254807.500	TAPR_126
TAPRTweety127	717213.563	4254807.500	TAPR_127
TAPRTweety128	710890.000	4254696.500	TAPR_128
TAPRTweety129	712332.188	4254696.500	TAPR_129
TAPRTweety130	715216.625	4254696.500	TAPR_130
TAPRTweety131	716658.875	4254696.500	TAPR_131
TAPRTweety132	710335.313	4254585.500	TAPR_132
TAPRTweety133	711777.500	4254585.500	TAPR_133
TAPRTweety134	716104.188	4254585.500	TAPR_134
TAPRTweety135	717546.375	4254585.500	TAPR_135
TAPRTweety136	711222.813	4254475.000	TAPR_136
TAPRTweety137	712665.063	4254475.000	TAPR_137
TAPRTweety138	715549.500	4254475.000	TAPR_138
TAPRTweety139	716991.688	4254475.000	TAPR_139
TAPRTweety140	710668.125	4254364.000	TAPR_140
TAPRTweety141	712110.313	4254364.000	TAPR_141
TAPRTweety142	716437.000	4254364.000	TAPR_142
TAPRTweety143	717879.188	4254364.000	TAPR_143
TAPRTweety144	710113.438	4254253.000	TAPR_144
TAPRTweety145	711555.625	4254253.000	TAPR_145
TAPRTweety146	712997.875	4254253.000	TAPR_146
TAPRTweety147	714440.063	4254253.000	TAPR_147
TAPRTweety148	715882.313	4254253.000	TAPR_148
TAPRTweety149	717324.500	4254253.000	TAPR_149
TAPRTweety150	711000.938	4254142.000	TAPR_150
TAPRTweety151	712443.125	4254142.000	TAPR_151
TAPRTweety152	715327.625	4254142.000	TAPR_152
TAPRTweety153	716769.813	4254142.000	TAPR_153
TAPRTweety154	710446.250	4254031.000	TAPR_154
TAPRTweety155	711888.438	4254031.000	TAPR_155
TAPRTweety156	716215.125	4254031.000	TAPR_156
TAPRTweety157	717657.313	4254031.000	TAPR_157
TAPRTweety158	712776.000	4253920.000	TAPR_158

Table B.10: continued

Plot I.D.	X Coordinate (Easting)	Y Coordinate (Northing)	Inventory I.D. Number
TAPRTweety159	710124.563	4263197.500	TAPR_159
TAPRTweety160	710595.688	4263155.500	TAPR_160
TAPRTweety161	711047.063	4263231.000	TAPR_161
TAPRTweety162	711485.500	4263098.000	TAPR_162
TAPRTweety163	711937.875	4263106.500	TAPR_163
TAPRTweety164	713868.747	4253532.017	TAPR_164
TAPRTweety165	713917.305	4253809.841	TAPR_165
TAPRTweety166	713812.750	4254043.000	TAPR_166
TAPRTweety167	714030.250	4254271.500	TAPR_167
TAPRTweety168	713809.000	4254492.500	TAPR_168
TAPRTweety169	713985.612	4254725.183	TAPR_169
TAPRTweety170	714108.110	4255143.297	TAPR_170
TAPRTweety171	714000.500	4255541.500	TAPR_171
TAPRTweety172	713937.750	4256031.000	TAPR_172
TAPRTweety173	713834.688	4256265.000	TAPR_173
TAPRTweety174	713867.938	4256715.000	TAPR_174
TAPRTweety175	713817.500	4257008.000	TAPR_175
TAPRTweety176	709815.813	4263404.000	TAPR_176
TAPRTweety177	711111.875	4263683.000	TAPR_177
TAPRTweety178	710557.188	4263572.000	TAPR_178
TAPRTweety179	711999.375	4263572.000	TAPR_179
TAPRTweety180	710002.500	4263461.000	TAPR_180
TAPRTweety181	710890.000	4263350.000	TAPR_181
TAPRTweety182	711777.500	4263239.000	TAPR_182
TAPRTweety183	710668.125	4263017.000	TAPR_183
TAPRTweety184	709669.625	4262240.500	TAPR_184
TAPRTweety185	712110.313	4261575.000	TAPR_185
TAPRTweety186	710113.438	4261464.000	TAPR_186
TAPRTweety187	711000.938	4261353.000	TAPR_187
TAPRTweety188	710446.250	4261242.000	TAPR_188
TAPRTweety189	711888.438	4261242.000	TAPR_189
TAPRTweety190	711333.750	4261131.000	TAPR_190
TAPRTweety191	712221.250	4261020.000	TAPR_191
TAPRTweety192	709669.625	4260798.500	TAPR_192
TAPRTweety193	709780.563	4260243.500	TAPR_193
TAPRTweety194	712110.313	4260132.500	TAPR_194
TAPRTweety195	712443.125	4259911.000	TAPR_195
TAPRTweety196	709780.563	4258801.500	TAPR_196
TAPRTweety197	710113.438	4258579.500	TAPR_197
TAPRTweety198	711555.625	4258579.500	TAPR_198
TAPRTweety199	712997.875	4258579.500	TAPR_199
TAPRTweety200	711000.938	4258468.500	TAPR_200
TAPRTweety201	712443.125	4258468.500	TAPR_201
TAPRTweety202	710446.250	4258357.500	TAPR_202
TAPRTweety203	711888.438	4258357.500	TAPR_203
TAPRTweety204	709891.563	4258246.500	TAPR_204
TAPRTweety205	712221.250	4258136.000	TAPR_205
TAPRTweety206	713108.813	4258025.000	TAPR_206
TAPRTweety207	712554.063	4257914.000	TAPR_207
TAPRTweety208	712332.188	4257581.000	TAPR_208
TAPRTweety209	709780.563	4257359.000	TAPR_209
TAPRTweety210	712665.063	4257359.000	TAPR_210
TAPRTweety211	712997.875	4257137.500	TAPR_ 211

Table B.10: continued

Plot I.D.	X Coordinate (Easting)	Y Coordinate (Northing)	Inventory I.D. Number
TAPRTweety212	714440.063	4257137.500	TAPR_212
TAPRTweety213	711000.938	4257026.500	TAPR_213
TAPRTweety214	712443.125	4257026.500	TAPR_214
TAPRTweety215	710446.250	4256915.500	TAPR_215
TAPRTweety216	711888.438	4256915.500	TAPR_216
TAPRTweety217	713330.688	4256915.500	TAPR_217
TAPRTweety218	709891.563	4256804.500	TAPR_218
TAPRTweety219	711333.750	4256804.500	TAPR_219
TAPRTweety220	712776.000	4256804.500	TAPR_220
TAPRTweety221	710779.063	4256693.500	TAPR_221
TAPRTweety222	712221.250	4256693.500	TAPR_222
TAPRTweety223	713108.813	4256582.500	TAPR_223
TAPRTweety224	712554.063	4256471.500	TAPR_224
TAPRTweety225	713441.625	4256360.500	TAPR_225
TAPRTweety226	712886.938	4256250.000	TAPR_226
TAPRTweety227	714661.938	4256028.000	TAPR_227
TAPRTweety228	709780.563	4255917.000	TAPR_228
TAPRTweety229	712665.063	4255917.000	TAPR_229
TAPRTweety230	714107.250	4255917.000	TAPR_230
TAPRTweety231	712997.875	4255695.000	TAPR_231
TAPRTweety232	713885.375	4255584.000	TAPR_232
TAPRTweety233	714772.875	4255473.000	TAPR_233
TAPRTweety234	709891.563	4255362.500	TAPR_234
TAPRTweety235	711333.750	4255362.500	TAPR_235
TAPRTweety236	712776.000	4255362.500	TAPR_236
TAPRTweety237	714218.188	4255362.500	TAPR_237
TAPRTweety238	717102.625	4255362.500	TAPR_238
TAPRTweety239	710779.063	4255251.500	TAPR_239
TAPRTweety240	712221.250	4255251.500	TAPR_240
TAPRTweety241	715105.688	4255251.500	TAPR_241
TAPRTweety242	716547.938	4255251.500	TAPR_242
TAPRTweety243	717990.125	4255251.500	TAPR_243
TAPRTweety244	710224.375	4255140.500	TAPR_244
TAPRTweety245	711666.563	4255140.500	TAPR_245
TAPRTweety246	713108.813	4255140.500	TAPR_246
TAPRTweety247	713441.625	4254918.500	TAPR_247
TAPRTweety248	714883.813	4254918.500	TAPR_248
TAPRTweety249	714661.938	4254585.500	TAPR_249
TAPRTweety250	713552.563	4254364.000	TAPR_250
TAPRTweety251	714994.750	4254364.000	TAPR_251
TAPRTweety252	714772.875	4254031.000	TAPR_252
TAPRTweety253	711333.750	4253920.000	TAPR_253
TAPRTweety254	714218.188	4253920.000	TAPR_254
TAPRTweety255	715660.438	4253920.000	TAPR_255
TAPRTweety256	717102.625	4253920.000	TAPR_256
TAPRTweety257	710779.063	4253809.000	TAPR_257
TAPRTweety258	712221.250	4253809.000	TAPR_258
TAPRTweety259	715105.688	4253809.000	TAPR_259
TAPRTweety260	714551.000	4253698.000	TAPR_260

Table B.11: Waypoints for Wilson's Creek National Battlefield, Missouri – UTM Zone 15 North, Datum 1983 (Conus).

Plot I.D.	X Coordinate (Easting)	Y Coordinate (Northing)	Inventory I.D. Number
WICRTweety1	462677.994	4108243.010	WICR_1
WICRTweety2	462960.837	4107960.167	WICR_2
WICRTweety3	463526.522	4107960.167	WICR_3
WICRTweety4	464092.207	4107960.167	WICR_4
WICRTweety5	462677.994	4107677.325	WICR_5
WICRTweety6	463243.679	4107677.325	WICR_6
WICRTweety7	463809.365	4107677.325	WICR_7
WICRTweety8	464375.050	4107677.325	WICR_8
WICRTweety9	462960.837	4107394.482	WICR_9
WICRTweety10	463526.522	4107394.482	WICR_10
WICRTweety11	464092.207	4107394.482	WICR_11
WICRTweety12	463243.679	4107111.639	WICR_12
WICRTweety13	463809.365	4107111.639	WICR_13
WICRTweety14	464375.050	4107111.639	WICR_14
WICRTweety15	463526.522	4106828.796	WICR_15
WICRTweety16	464092.207	4106828.796	WICR_16
WICRTweety17	463243.679	4106545.954	WICR_17
WICRTweety18	463809.365	4106545.954	WICR_18
WICRTweety19	464375.050	4106545.954	WICR_19
WICRTweety20	463526.522	4106263.111	WICR_20
WICRTweety21	464092.207	4106263.111	WICR_21
WICRTweety22	463243.679	4105980.268	WICR_22
WICRTweety23	463809.365	4105980.268	WICR_23
WICRTweety24	464375.050	4105980.268	WICR_24
WICRTweety25	463526.522	4105697.426	WICR_25
WICRTweety26	464092.207	4105697.426	WICR_26
WICRTweety27	463243.679	4105414.583	WICR_27
WICRTweety28	463809.365	4105414.583	WICR_28
WICRTweety29	464375.050	4105414.583	WICR_29
WICRTweety30	463526.522	4105131.740	WICR_30
WICRTweety31	463243.679	4104848.897	WICR_31
WICRTweety32	463809.365	4104848.897	WICR_32
WICRTweety33	464375.050	4104848.897	WICR_33
WICRTweety34	463526.522	4104566.055	WICR_34
WICRTweety35	464092.207	4104566.055	WICR_35
WICRTweety36	463243.679	4104283.212	WICR_36
WICRTweety37	464375.050	4104283.212	WICR_37
WICRTweety38	462395.151	4104000.369	WICR_38

Appendix C. Bird Species Lists for Heartland Network, by Park

Table C.1: Bird List for Arkansas Post National Memorial, Arkansas.

Common Name	AOU Code	Common Name	AOU Code
Acadian Flycatcher	ACFL	Eastern Towhee	EATO
American Coot	AMCO	Eastern Wood-pewee	EAWP
American Crow	AMCR	European Starling	EUST
American Goldfinch	AMGO	Field Sparrow	FISP
American Kestrel	AMKE	Fish Crow	FICR
American Redstart	AMRE	Fox Sparrow	FOSP
American Robin	AMRO	Gadwall	GADW
American Woodcock	AMWO	Glossy Ibis	GLIB
Anhinga	ANHI	Golden-winged Warbler	GWWA
Bachman's Sparrow	BACS	Grasshopper Sparrow	GRSP
Bald Eagle	BAEA	Gray Catbird	GRCA
Barn Owl	BNOW	Great Blue Heron	GBHE
Barn Swallow	BARS	Great Crested Flycatcher	GCFL
Barred Owl	BDOW	Great Egret	GREG
Bell's Vireo	BEVI	Great Horned Owl	GHOW
Belted Kingbird	BEKI	Green Heron	GRHE
Black Vulture	BLVU	Hairy Woodpecker	HAWO
Black-and-White Warbler	BAWW	Hooded Merganser	HOME
Black-crowned Night Heron	BCNH	Hooded Warbler	HOWA
Blue Grosbeak	BLGR	Horned Lark	HOLA
Blue Jay	BLJA	House Finch	HOFI
Blue-gray Gnatcatcher	BGGN	House Sparrow	HOSP
Blue-winged Warbler	BWWA	House Wren	HOWR
Brown Thrasher	BRTH	Indigo Bunting	INBU
Brown-headed Cowbird	BHCO	Kentucky Warbler	KEWA
Brown-headed Nuthatch	BHNU	Killdeer	KILL
Canada Goose	CAGO	King Rail	KIRA
Carolina Chickadee	CACH	Lark Sparrow	LASP
Carolina Wren	CARW	Least Bittern	LEBI
Cattle Egret	CAEG	Least Tern	LETE
Cerulean Warbler	CERW	Little Blue Heron	LBHE
Chimney Swift	CHSW	Loggerhead Shrike	LOSH
Chipping Sparrow	CHSP	Louisiana Waterthrush	LOWA
Chuck-will's-widow	CWWI	Mallard	MALL
Cliff Swallow	CLSW	Mourning Dove	MODO
Common Golden-eye	COGO	Northern Bobwhite	NOBO
Common Grackle	COGR	Northern Cardinal	NOCA
Common Morehead	COMO	Northern Flicker	YSFL
Common Nighthawk	CONI	Northern Mockingbird	NOMO
Common Yellowthroat	COYE	Northern Oriole	BAOR
Cooper's Hawk	COHA	Northern Parula	NOPA
Dickcissel	DICK	Northern Pintail	NOPI
Double-crested Cormorant	DCCO	Northern Rough-winged Swallow	NRWS
Downy Woodpecker	DOWO	Northern Shoveler	NSHO
Eastern Bluebird	EABL	Orchard Oriole	OROR
Eastern Kingbird	EAKI	Ovenbird	OVEN
Eastern Meadowlark	EAME	Pied-billed Grebe	PBGR
Eastern Phoebe	EAPH	Pileated Woodpecker	PIWO
Eastern Screech Owl	EASO	Pine Warbler	PIWA

Table C.1: Bird List for Arkansas Post National Memorial, Arkansas - continued.

Common Name	AOU Code	Common Name	AOU Code
Prairie Warbler	PRAW	Turkey Vulture	TUVU
Prothonotary Warbler	PROW	Warbling Vireo	WAVI
Purple Finch	PUFI	Whip-poor-will	WPWI
Purple Gallinule	PUGA	White Ibis	WHIB
Purple Martin	PUMA	White-breasted Nuthatch	WBNU
Red-bellied Woodpecker	RBWO	White-eyed Vireo	WEVI
Red-eyed Vireo	REVI	White-faced Ibis	WFIB
Red-headed Woodpecker	RHWO	Wild Turkey	WITU
Red-shouldered Hawk	RSHA	Wood Duck	WODU
Red-tailed Hawk	RTHA	Wood Stork	WOST
Red-winged Blackbird	RWBL	Wood Thrush	WOTH
Rock Dove	RODO	Yellow Warbler	YWAR
Rose-breasted Grosbeak	RBGR	Yellow-billed Cuckoo	YBCU
Ruby-throated Hummingbird	RTHU	Yellow-breasted Chat	YBCH
Snowy Egret	SNEG	Yellow-crowned Night Heron	YCNH
Summer Tanager	SUTA	Yellow-throated Vireo	YTVI
Swainson's Warbler	SWWA	Yellow-throated Warbler	YTWA
Tuffed Titmouse	ETTI		

Table C.2: Bird List for Effigy Mounds National Monument, Iowa.

Common Name	AOU Code	Common Name	AOU Code
Acadian Flycatcher	ACFL	Eastern Wood-pewee	EAWP
American Bittern	AMBI	European Starling	EUST
American Coot	AMCO	Field Sparrow	FISP
American Crow	AMCR	Gadwall	GADW
American Goldfinch	AMGO	Golden-winged Warbler	GWWA
American Kestrel	AMKE	Grasshopper Sparrow	GRSP
American Redstart	AMRE	Gray Catbird	GRCA
American Robin	AMRO	Gray Partridge	GRPA
American Woodcock	AMWO	Great Blue Heron	GBHE
Bald Eagle	BAEA	Great Crested Flycatcher	GCFL
Bank Swallow	BANS	Great Egret	GREG
Barn Owl	BNOW	Great Horned Owl	GHOW
Barn Swallow	BARS	Green Heron	GRHE
Barred Owl	BDOW	Hairy Woodpecker	HAWO
Belted Kingbird	BEKI	Henslow's Sparrow	HESP
Black-and-White Warbler	BAWW	Hooded Merganser	HOME
Black-billed Cuckoo	BBCU	Hooded Warbler	HOWA
Black-capped Chickadee	BCCH	Horned Lark	HOLA
Black-crowned Night Heron	BCNH	House Finch	HOFI
Black-tern	BLTE	House Sparrow	HOSP
Blue Grosbeak	BLGR	House Wren	HOWR
Blue Jay	BLJA	Indigo Bunting	INBU
Blue-gray Gnatcatcher	BGGN	Kentucky Warbler	KEWA
Blue-winged Teal	BWTE	Killdeer	KILL
Blue-winged Warbler	BWWA	King Rail	KIRA
Broad-winged Hawk	BWHA	Lark Sparrow	LASP
Brown Creeper	BRCR	Least Bittern	LEBI
Brown Thrasher	BRTH	Least Flycatcher	LEFL
Brown-headed Cowbird	BHCO	Little Blue Heron	LBHE
Canada Goose	CAGO	Loggerhead Shrike	LOSH
Carolina Wren	CARW	Long-eared Owl	LEOW
Cattle Egret	CAEG	Louisiana Waterthrush	LOWA
Cedar Waxwing	CEDW	Mallard	MALL
Cerulean Warbler	CERW	Marsh Wren	MAWR
Chestnut-sided Warbler	CSWA	Mourning Dove	MODO
Chimney Swift	CHSW	Northern Bobwhite	NOBO
Chipping Sparrow	CHSP	Northern Cardinal	NOCA
Cliff Swallow	CLSW	Northern Flicker	YSFL
Common Grackle	COGR	Northern Harrier	NOHA
Common Morehead	COMO	Northern Mockingbird	NOMO
Common Nighthawk	CONI	Northern Oriole	BAOR
Common Snipe	COSN	Northern Parula	NOPA
Common Yellowthroat	COYE	Northern Pintail	NOPI
Cooper's Hawk	COHA	Northern Rough-winged Swallow	NRWS
Dark-eyed Junco	SCJU	Northern Shoveler	NSHO
Dickcissel	DICK	Northern Waterthrush	NOWA
Double-crested Cormorant	DCCO	Northern Saw-whet Owl	NSWO
Downy Woodpecker	DOWO	Orchard Oriole	OROR
Eastern Bluebird	EABL	Ovenbird	OVEN
Eastern Kingbird	EAKI	Pied-billed Grebe	PBGR
Eastern Meadowlark	EAME	Pileated Woodpecker	PIWO
Eastern Phoebe	EAPH	Prothonotary Warbler	PROW
Eastern Screech Owl	EASO	Purple Finch	PUFI
Eastern Towhee	EATO	Purple Martin	PUMA

Table C.2: Bird List for Effigy Mounds National Monument, Iowa - continued.

Common Name	AOU Code	Common Name	AOU Code
Red-bellied Woodpecker	RBWO	Tufted Titmouse	ETTI
Red-eyed Vireo	REVI	Turkey Vulture	TUVU
Redhead	REDH	Upland Sandpiper	UPSA
Red-headed Woodpecker	RHWO	Veery	VEER
Red-shouldered Hawk	RSHA	Vesper Sparrow	VESP
Red-tailed Hawk	RTHA	Virginia Rail	VIRA
Red-winged Blackbird	RWBL	Warbling Vireo	WAVI
Ring-necked Duck	RNDU	Western Meadowlark	WEME
Ring-necked Pheasant	RPHE	Whip-poor-will	WPWI
Rock Dove	RODO	White Ibis	WHIB
Rose-breasted Grosbeak	RBGR	White-breasted Nuthatch	WBNU
Ruby-throated Hummingbird	RTHU	White-faced Ibis	WFIB
Ruddy Duck	RUDU	Wild Turkey	WITU
Ruffed Grouse	RUGR	Willow Flycatcher	WIFL
Savannah Sparrow	SAVS	Wood Duck	WODU
Scarlet Tanager	SCTA	Wood Thrush	WOTH
Sedge Wren	SEWR	Worm-eating Warbler	WEWA
Sharp-shinned Hawk	SSHA	Yellow Rail	YERA
Short-eared Owl	SEOW	Yellow Warbler	YWAR
Snowy Egret	SNEG	Yellow-bellied Sapsucker	YBSA
Song Sparrow	SOSP	Yellow-billed Cuckoo	YBCU
Sora	SORA	Yellow-breasted Chat	YBCH
Spotted Sandpiper	SPSA	Yellow-crowned Night Heron	YCNH
Swamp Sparrow	SWSP	Yellow-headed Blackbird	YHBL
Tree Swallow	TRES	Yellow-throated Vireo	YTVI

Table C.3: Bird List for George Washington Carver National Monument, Missouri.

Common Name	AOU Code	Common Name	AOU Code
Acadian Flycatcher	ACFL	Green Heron	GRHE
American Crow	AMCR	Hairy Woodpecker	HAWO
American Goldfinch	AMGO	Hooded Merganser	HOME
American Kestrel	AMKE	Hooded Warbler	HOWA
American Redstart	AMRE	Horned Lark	HOLA
American Robin	AMRO	House Finch	HOFI
American Woodcock	AMWO	House Sparrow	HOSP
Bank Swallow	BANS	House Wren	HOWR
Barn Owl	BNOW	Indigo Bunting	INBU
Barn Swallow	BARS	Kentucky Warbler	KEWA
Barred Owl	BDOW	Killdeer	KILL
Bell's Vireo	BEVI	Lark Sparrow	LASP
Belted Kingbird	BEKI	Loggerhead Shrike	LOSH
Bewick's Wren	BEWR	Long-eared Owl	LEOW
Black-and-White Warbler	BAWW	Mallard	MALL
Black-billed Cuckoo	BBCU	Mourning Dove	MODO
Black-crowned Night Heron	BCNH	Northern Bobwhite	NOBO
Blue Grosbeak	BLGR	Northern Cardinal	NOCA
Blue Jay	BLJA	Northern Flicker	YSFL
Blue-gray Gnatcatcher	BGGN	Northern Harrier	NOHA
Blue-winged Teal	BWTE	Northern Mockingbird	NOMO
Blue-winged Warbler	BWWA	Northern Oriole	BAOR
Brown Thrasher	BRTH	Northern Parula	NOPA
Brown-headed Cowbird	BHCO	Northern Rough-winged Swallow	NRWS
Canada Goose	CAGO	Orchard Oriole	OROR
Carolina Chickadee	CACH	Painted Bunting	PABU
Carolina Wren	CARW	Pileated Woodpecker	PIWO
Cattle Egret	CAEG	Pine Warbler	PIWA
Cerulean Warbler	CERW	Prairie Warbler	PRAW
Chimney Swift	CHSW	Prothonotary Warbler	PROW
Chipping Sparrow	CHSP	Purple Finch	PUFI
Chuck-will's-widow	CWWI	Purple Martin	PUMA
Cliff Swallow	CLSW	Red-bellied Woodpecker	RBWO
Common Grackle	COGR	Red-eyed Vireo	REVI
Common Nighthawk	CONI	Red-headed Woodpecker	RHWO
Common Yellowthroat	COYE	Red-shouldered Hawk	RSHA
Dickcissel	DICK	Red-tailed Hawk	RTHA
Downy Woodpecker	DOWO	Red-winged Blackbird	RWBL
Eastern Bluebird	EABL	Rock Dove	RODO
Eastern Kingbird	EAKI	Rose-breasted Grosbeak	RBGR
Eastern Meadowlark	EAME	Ruby-throated Hummingbird	RTHU
Eastern Phoebe	EAPH	Scarlet Tanager	SCTA
Eastern Screech-Owl	EASO	Song Sparrow	SOSP
Eastern Towhee	EATO	Summer Tanager	SUTA
Eastern Wood-Pewee	EAWP	Tree Swallow	TRES
European Starling	EUST	Tuffed Titmouse	ETTI
Field Sparrow	FISP	Turkey Vulture	TUVU
Golden-winged Warbler	GWWA	Warbling Vireo	WAVI
Grasshopper Sparrow	GRSP	Whip-poor-will	WPWI
Gray Catbird	GRCA	White-eyed Vireo	WEVI
Great Blue Heron	GBHE	Willow Flycatcher	WIFL
Great Crested Flycatcher	GCFL	Wood Duck	WODU
Great Horned Owl	GHOW	Wood Thrush	WOTH
Greater Roadrunner	GRRO	Yellow Warbler	YWAR

Table C.3: Bird List for George Washington Carver National Monument, Missouri - continued.

Common Name	AOU Code	Common Name	AOU Code
Yellow-billed Cuckoo	YBCU	Yellow-throated Vireo	YTVI
Yellow-breasted Chat	YBCH	Yellow-throated Warbler	YTWA
Yellow-crowned Night Heron	YCNH		

Table C.4: Bird List for Herbert Hoover National Historic Site, Iowa.

Common Name	AOU Code	Common Name	AOU Code
Acadian Flycatcher	ACFL	House Wren	HOWR
American Bittern	AMBI	Indigo Bunting	INBU
American Crow	AMCR	Killdeer	KILL
American Goldfinch	AMGO	Lark Sparrow	LASP
(American) Green-winged Teal	AGWT	Least Bittern	LEBI
American Kestrel	AMKE	Least Flycatcher	LEFL
American Redstart	AMRE	Loggerhead Shrike	LOSH
American Robin	AMRO	Long-eared Owl	LEOW
Bald Eagle	BAEA	Mallard	MALL
Bank Swallow	BANS	Marsh Wren	MAWR
Barn Owl	BNOW	Mourning Dove	MODO
Barn Swallow	BARS	Northern Bobwhite	NOBO
Barred Owl	BDOW	Northern Cardinal	NOCA
Bell's Vireo	BEVI	Northern Flicker	YSFL
Belted Kingbird	BEKI	Northern Harrier	NOHA
Black-billed Cuckoo	BBCU	Northern Mockingbird	NOMO
Black-capped Chickadee	BCCH	Northern Oriole	BAOR
Blue Grosbeak	BLGR	Northern Rough-winged Swallow	NRWS
Blue Jay	BLJA	Northern Saw-whet Owl	NSWO
Brown Creeper	BRCR	Orchard Oriole	OROR
Brown Thrasher	BRTH	Pileated Woodpecker	PIWO
Brown-headed Cowbird	BHCO	Purple Finch	PUFI
Canada Goose	CAGO	Purple Martin	PUMA
Carolina Wren	CARW	Red-bellied Woodpecker	RBWO
Cattle Egret	CAEG	Red-eyed Vireo	REVI
Cedar Waxwing	CEDW	Red-headed Woodpecker	RHWO
Chimney Swift	CHSW	Red-tailed Hawk	RTHA
Chipping Sparrow	CHSP	Red-winged Blackbird	RWBL
Cliff Swallow	CLSW	Ring-necked Pheasant	RPHE
Common Grackle	COGR	Rock Dove	RODO
Common Nighthawk	CONI	Rose-breasted Grosbeak	RBGR
Common Yellowthroat	COYE	Ruby-throated Hummingbird	RTHU
Dickcissel	DICK	Savannah Sparrow	SAVS
Double-crested Cormorant	DCCO	Scissor-tailed Flycatcher	STFL
Downy Woodpecker	DOWO	Sedge Wren	SEWR
Eastern Bluebird	EABL	Short-eared Owl	SEOW
Eastern Kingbird	EAKI	Song Sparrow	SOSP
Eastern Meadowlark	EAME	Swamp Sparrow	SWSP
Eastern Phoebe	EAPH	Tree Swallow	TRES
Eastern Screech Owl	EASO	Tuffed Titmouse	ETTI
Eastern Towhee	EATO	Turkey Vulture	TUVU
Eastern Wood-Pewee	EAWP	Upland Sandpiper	UPSA
European Starling	EUST	Vesper Sparrow	VESP
Field Sparrow	FISP	Warbling Vireo	WAVI
Grasshopper Sparrow	GRSP	Western Meadowlark	WEME
Gray Catbird	GRCA	White-breasted Nuthatch	WBNU
Great Blue Heron	GBHE	White-crowned Sparrow	WCSP
Great Crested Flycatcher	GCFL	Wild Turkey	WITU
Great Horned Owl	GHOW	Wood Duck	WODU
Hairy Woodpecker	HAWO	Yellow Warbler	YWAR
Henslow's Sparrow	HESP	Yellow-bellied Sapsucker	YBSA
Horned Lark	HOLA	Yellow-billed Cuckoo	YBCU
House Finch	HOFI	Yellow-rumped Warbler	MYWA
House Sparrow	HOSP		

Table C.5: Bird List for Homestead National Monument of America, Nebraska.

Common Name	AOU Code	Common Name	AOU Code
Acadian Flycatcher	ACFL	Indigo Bunting	INBU
American Crow	AMCR	Killdeer	KILL
American Goldfinch	AMGO	Lark Bunting	LARB
American Kestrel	AMKE	Lark Sparrow	LASP
American Redstart	AMRE	Least Flycatcher	LEFL
American Robin	AMRO	Loggerhead Shrike	LOSH
Bank Swallow	BANS	Long-eared Owl	LEOW
Barn Owl	BNOW	Mallard	MALL
Barn Swallow	BARS	Marsh Wren	MAWR
Barred Owl	BDOW	Mourning Dove	MODO
Bell's Vireo	BEVI	Northern Bobwhite	NOBO
Black-and-White Warbler	BAWW	Northern Cardinal	NOCA
Black-billed Cuckoo	BBCU	Northern Flicker	YSFL
Black-capped Chickadee	BCCH	Northern Harrier	NOHA
Black-crowned Night Heron	BCNH	Northern Mockingbird	NOMO
Blue Grosbeak	BLGR	Northern Oriole	BAOR
Blue Jay	BLJA	Northern Rough-winged Swallow	NRWS
Blue-winged Teal	BWTE	Orchard Oriole	OROR
Brown Thrasher	BRTH	Osprey	OSPR
Brown-headed Cowbird	BHCO	Pileated Woodpecker	PIWO
Burrowing Owl	BUOW	Pine Warbler	PIWA
Canada Goose	CAGO	Purple Finch	PUFI
Carolina Wren	CARW	Purple Martin	PUMA
Cattle Egret	CAEG	Red-bellied Woodpecker	RBWO
Cedar Waxwing	CEDW	Red-eyed Vireo	REVI
Chimney Swift	CHSW	Red-headed Woodpecker	RHWO
Chipping Sparrow	CHSP	Red-shouldered Hawk	RSHA
Cliff Swallow	CLSW	Red-tailed Hawk	RTHA
Common Grackle	COGR	Red-winged Blackbird	RWBL
Common Nighthawk	CONI	Ring-necked Pheasant	RPHE
Common Yellowthroat	COYE	Rock Dove	RODO
Dickcissel	DICK	Rose-breasted Grosbeak	RBGR
Downy Woodpecker	DOWO	Ruby-throated Hummingbird	RTHU
Eastern Bluebird	EABL	Savannah Sparrow	SAVS
Eastern Kingbird	EAKI	Scissor-tailed Flycatcher	STFL
Eastern Meadowlark	EAME	Short-eared Owl	SEOW
Eastern Phoebe	EAPH	Song Sparrow	SOSP
Eastern Screech Owl	EASO	Spotted Sandpiper	SPSA
Eastern Towhee	EATO	Swainson's Hawk	SWHA
Eastern Wood-pewee	EAWP	Swamp Sparrow	SWSP
European Starling	EUST	Tree Swallow	TRES
Field Sparrow	FISP	Tuffed Titmouse	ETTI
Grasshopper Sparrow	GRSP	Turkey Vulture	TUVU
Gray Catbird	GRCA	Upland Sandpiper	UPSA
Great Blue Heron	GBHE	Vesper Sparrow	VESP
Great Crested Flycatcher	GCFL	Warbling Vireo	WAVI
Great Horned Owl	GHOW	Western Kingbird	WEKI
Green Heron	GRHE	Western Meadowlark	WEME
Hairy Woodpecker	HAWO	White-breasted Nuthatch	WBNU
Henslow's Sparrow	HESP	White-eyed Vireo	WEVI
Horned Lark	HOLA	Wild Turkey	WITU
House Finch	HOFI	Willow Flycatcher	WIFL
House Sparrow	HOSP	Wood Thrush	WOTH
House Wren	HOWR	Wood Duck	WODU

Table C.5: Bird List for Homestead National Monument of America, Nebraska - continued.

Common Name	AOU Code	Common Name	AOU Code
Yellow Warbler	YWAR	Yellow-breasted Chat	YBCH
Yellow-bellied Sapsucker	YBSA	Yellow-crowned Night Heron	YCNH
Yellow-billed Cuckoo	YBCU	Yellow-throated Vireo	YTVI

Table C.6: Bird List for Hopewell Cultural National Historical Park, Ohio.

Common Name	AOU Code	Common Name	AOU Code
Acadian Flycatcher	ACFL	Common Nighthawk	CONI
American Black Duck	ABDU	Common Yellowthroat	COYE
American Coot	AMCO	Cooper's Hawk	COHA
American Crow	AMCR	Dark-eyed Junco	SCJU
American Goldfinch	AMGO	Dickcissel	DICK
American Kestrel	AMKE	Double-crested Cormorant	DCCO
American Pipit	AMPI	Downy Woodpecker	DOWO
American Redstart	AMRE	Dunlin	DUNL
American Robin	AMRO	Eastern Bluebird	EABL
American Tree Sparrow	ATSP	Eastern Kingbird	EAKI
American Woodcock	AMWO	Eastern Meadowlark	EAME
Bachman's Sparrow	BACS	Eastern Phoebe	EAPH
Bald Eagle	BAEA	Eastern Screech Owl	EASO
Bank Swallow	BANS	Eastern Towhee	EATO
Barn Owl	BNOW	Eastern Wood-Pewee	EAWP
Barn Swallow	BARS	European Starling	EUST
Barred Owl	BDOW	Field Sparrow	FISP
Bay-breasted Warbler	BBWA	Fox Sparrow	FOSP
Bell's Vireo	BEVI	Golden-crowned Kinglet	GCKI
Belted Kingbird	BEKI	Golden-winged Warbler	GWWA
Bewick's Wren	BEWR	Grasshopper Sparrow	GRSP
Black Vulture	BLVU	Gray Catbird	GRCA
Black-and-White Warbler	BAWW	Gray-cheeked Thrush	GCTH
Black-billed Cuckoo	BBCU	Great Blue Heron	GBHE
Blackburnian Warbler	BLBW	Great Crested Flycatcher	GCFL
Black-capped Chickadee	BCCH	Great Egret	GREG
Blackpoll Warbler	BLPW	Great Horned Owl	GHOW
Black-throated Blue Warbler	BTBW	Green Heron	GRHE
Black-throated Green Warbler	BTNW	Hairy Woodpecker	HAWO
Blue Grosbeak	BLGR	Henslow's Sparrow	HESP
Blue Jay	BLJA	Hermit Thrush	HETH
Blue-gray Gnatcatcher	BGGN	Hooded Merganser	HOME
Blue-winged Teal	BWTE	Hooded Warbler	HOWA
Blue-winged Warbler	BWWA	Horned Lark	HOLA
Broad-winged Hawk	BWHA	House Finch	HOFI
Brown Creeper	BRCR	House Sparrow	HOSP
Brown Thrasher	BRTH	House Wren	HOWR
Brown-headed Cowbird	BHCO	Indigo Bunting	INBU
Canada Goose	CAGO	Kentucky Warbler	KEWA
Canada Warbler	CAWA	Killdeer	KILL
Cape May Warbler	CMWA	Lark Sparrow	LASP
Carolina Chickadee	CACH	Least Flycatcher	LEFL
Carolina Wren	CARW	Lesser Scaup	LESC
Caspian Tern	CATE	Little Blue Heron	LBHE
Cattle Egret	CAEG	Loggerhead Shrike	LOSH
Cedar Waxwing	CEDW	Long-eared Owl	LEOW
Cerulean Warbler	CERW	Magnolia Warbler	MAWA
Chestnut-sided Warbler	CSWA	Mallard	MALL
Chimney Swift	CHSW	Marsh Wren	MAWR
Chipping Sparrow	CHSP	Mourning Dove	MODO
Cliff Swallow	CLSW	Northern Bobwhite	NOBO
Common Golden-eye	COGO	Northern Cardinal	NOCA
Common Grackle	COGR	Northern Flicker	YSFL
Common Merganser	COME	Northern Harrier	NOHA

Table C.6: Bird List for Hopewell Cultural National Historical Park, Ohio - continued.

Common Name	AOU Code	Common Name	AOU Code
Northern Mockingbird	NOMO	Sedge Wren	SEWR
Northern Oriole	BAOR	Sharp-shinned Hawk	SSHA
Northern Parula	NOPA	Snowy Egret	SNEG
Northern Pintail	NOPI	Solitary Sandpiper	SOSA
Northern Rough-winged Swallow	NRWS	Solitary Vireo	SOVI
Northern Waterthrush	NOWA	Song Sparrow	SOSP
Orchard Oriole	OROR	Spotted Sandpiper	SPSA
Osprey	OSPR	Summer Tanager	SUTA
Ovenbird	OVEN	Swainson's Thrush	SWTH
Palm Warbler	PAWA	Swamp Sparrow	SWSP
Philadelphia Vireo	PHVI	Tennessee Warbler	TEWA
Pied-billed Grebe	PBGR	Tree Swallow	TRES
Pileated Woodpecker	PIWO	Tuffed Titmouse	ETTI
Pine Warbler	PIWA	Turkey Vulture	TUVU
Prairie Warbler	PRAW	Upland Sandpiper	UPSA
Prothonotary Warbler	PROW	Veery	VEER
Purple Finch	PUFI	Vesper Sparrow	VESP
Purple Martin	PUMA	Warbling Vireo	WAVI
Red-bellied Woodpecker	RBWO	Western Meadowlark	WEME
Red-breasted Merganser	RBME	Whip-poor-will	WPWI
Red-breasted Nuthatch	RBNU	White-breasted Nuthatch	WBNU
Red-eyed Vireo	REVI	White-crowned Sparrow	WCSP
Redhead	REDH	White-eyed Vireo	WEVI
Red-headed Woodpecker	RHWO	White-throated Sparrow	WTSP
Red-necked Phalarope	RNPH	Wild Turkey	WITU
Red-shouldered Hawk	RSHA	Willow Flycatcher	WIFL
Red-tailed Hawk	RTHA	Wilson's Phalarope	WIPH
Red-winged Blackbird	RWBL	Wilson's Warbler	WIWA
Ring-billed Gull	RBGU	Winter Wren	WIWR
Ring-necked Duck	RNDU	Wood Duck	WODU
Ring-necked Pheasant	RPHE	Wood Thrush	WOTH
Rock Dove	RODO	Worm-eating Warbler	WEWA
Rose-breasted Grosbeak	RBGR	Yellow Warbler	YWAR
Rough-legged Hawk	RLHA	Yellow-bellied Flycatcher	YBFL
Ruby-crowned Kinglet	RCKI	Yellow-bellied Sapsucker	YBSA
Ruby-throated Hummingbird	RTHU	Yellow-billed Cuckoo	YBCU
Ruffed Grouse	RUGR	Yellow-breasted Chat	YBCH
Savannah Sparrow	SAVS	Yellow-throated Vireo	YTVI
Scarlet Tanager	SCTA	Yellow-throated Warbler	YTWA

Table C.7: Bird List for Lincoln Boyhood National Memorial, Indiana.

Common Name	AOU Code	Common Name	AOU Code
Acadian Flycatcher	ACFL	House Sparrow	HOSP
American Crow	AMCR	House Wren	HOWR
American Goldfinch	AMGO	Indigo Bunting	INBU
American Kestrel	AMKE	Kentucky Warbler	KEWA
American Redstart	AMRE	Killdeer	KILL
American Robin	AMRO	Lark Sparrow	LASP
American Woodcock	AMWO	Loggerhead Shrike	LOSH
Barn Owl	BNOW	Long-eared Owl	LEOW
Barn Swallow	BARS	Mourning Dove	MODO
Barred Owl	BDOW	Northern Bobwhite	NOBO
Bell's Vireo	BEVI	Northern Cardinal	NOCA
Bewick's Wren	BEWR	Northern Flicker	YSFL
Black Vulture	BLVU	Northern Mockingbird	NOMO
Black-and-White Warbler	BAWW	Northern Oriole	BAOR
Black-billed Cuckoo	BBCU	Northern Parula	NOPA
Blue Grosbeak	BLGR	Orchard Oriole	OROR
Blue Jay	BLJA	Ovenbird	OVEN
Blue-gray Gnatcatcher	BGGN	Pileated Woodpecker	PIWO
Blue-winged Warbler	BWWA	Pine Warbler	PIWA
Broad-winged Hawk	BWHA	Prairie Warbler	PRAW
Brown Thrasher	BRTH	Prothonotary Warbler	PROW
Brown-headed Cowbird	BHCO	Purple Finch	PUFI
Canada Goose	CAGO	Purple Martin	PUMA
Carolina Chickadee	CACH	Red-bellied Woodpecker	RBWO
Carolina Wren	CARW	Red-eyed Vireo	REVI
Chimney Swift	CHSW	Red-headed Woodpecker	RHWO
Chipping Sparrow	CHSP	Red-shouldered Hawk	RSHA
Chuck-will's-widow	CWWI	Red-tailed Hawk	RTHA
Cliff Swallow	CLSW	Red-winged Blackbird	RWBL
Common Grackle	COGR	Rock Dove	RODO
Common Nighthawk	CONI	Ruby-throated Hummingbird	RTHU
Common Yellowthroat	COYE	Ruffed Grouse	RUGR
Cooper's Hawk	COHA	Scarlet Tanager	SCTA
Dickcissel	DICK	Sharp-shinned Hawk	SSHA
Downy Woodpecker	DOWO	Summer Tanager	SUTA
Eastern Bluebird	EABL	Tree Swallow	TRES
Eastern Kingbird	EAKI	Tuffed Titmouse	ETTI
Eastern Meadowlark	EAME	Turkey Vulture	TUVU
Eastern Phoebe	EAPH	Warbling Vireo	WAVI
Eastern Screech Owl	EASO	Western Meadowlark	WEME
Eastern Towhee	EATO	Whip-poor-will	WPWI
Eastern Wood-Pewee	EAWP	White-breasted Nuthatch	WBNU
European Starling	EUST	White-eyed Vireo	WEVI
Field Sparrow	FISP	Wild Turkey	WITU
Golden-winged Warbler	GWWA	Willow Flycatcher	WIFL
Grasshopper Sparrow	GRSP	Wood Thrush	WOTH
Gray Catbird	GRCA	Worm-eating Warbler	WEWA
Great Crested Flycatcher	GCFL	Yellow Warbler	YWAR
Great Horned Owl	GHOW	Yellow-billed Cuckoo	YBCU
Hairy Woodpecker	HAWO	Yellow-breasted Chat	YBCH
Horned Lark	HOLA	Yellow-throated Vireo	YTVI
House Finch	HOFI	Yellow-throated Warbler	YTWA

Table C.8: Bird List for Pea Ridge National Military Park, Arkansas.

Common Name	AOU Code	Common Name	AOU Code
Acadian Flycatcher	ACFL	House Sparrow	HOSP
American Crow	AMCR	House Wren	HOWR
American Goldfinch	AMGO	Indigo Bunting	INBU
American Kestrel	AMKE	Kentucky Warbler	KEWA
American Redstart	AMRE	Killdeer	KILL
American Robin	AMRO	Lark Sparrow	LASP
American Woodcock	AMWO	Loggerhead Shrike	LOSH
Barn Owl	BNOW	Long-eared Owl	LEOW
Barn Swallow	BARS	Louisiana Waterthrush	LOWA
Barred Owl	BDOW	Mourning Dove	MODO
Bell's Vireo	BEVI	Northern Bobwhite	NOBO
Bewick's Wren	BEWR	Northern Cardinal	NOCA
Black-and-White Warbler	BAWW	Northern Flicker	NOFL
Black-billed Cuckoo	BBCU	Northern Harrier	NOHA
Blue Grosbeak	BLGR	Northern Mockingbird	NOMO
Blue Jay	BLJA	Northern Oriole	BAOR
Blue-gray Gnatcatcher	BGGN	Northern Parula	NOPA
Blue-winged Warbler	BWWA	Orchard Oriole	OROR
Broad-winged Hawk	BWHA	Ovenbird	OVEN
Brown Thrasher	BRTH	Painted Bunting	PABU
Brown-headed Cowbird	BHCO	Pileated Woodpecker	PIWO
Canada Goose	CAGO	Pine Warbler	PIWA
Carolina Chickadee	CACH	Prairie Warbler	PRAW
Carolina Wren	CARW	Purple Finch	PUFI
Cattle Egret	CAEG	Purple Martin	PUMA
Chimney Swift	CHSW	Red-bellied Woodpecker	RBWO
Chipping Sparrow	CHSP	Red-eyed Vireo	REVI
Chuck-will's-widow	CWWI	Red-headed Woodpecker	RHWO
Cliff Swallow	CLSW	Red-shouldered Hawk	RSHA
Common Grackle	COGR	Red-tailed Hawk	RTHA
Common Nighthawk	CONI	Red-winged Blackbird	RWBL
Common Yellowthroat	COYE	Rock Dove	RODO
Dickcissel	DICK	Rose-breasted Grosbeak	RBGR
Downy Woodpecker	DOWO	Ruby-throated Hummingbird	RTHU
Eastern Bluebird	EABL	Scarlet Tanager	SCTA
Eastern Kingbird	EAKI	Scissor-tailed Flycatcher	STFL
Eastern Meadowlark	EAME	Summer Tanager	SUTA
Eastern Phoebe	EAPH	Tree Swallow	TRES
Eastern Screech Owl	EASO	Tuffed Titmouse	ETTI
Eastern Towhee	EATO	Turkey Vulture	TUVU
Eastern Wood-Pewee	EAWP	Warbling Vireo	WAVI
European Starling	EUST	Whip-poor-will	WPWI
Field Sparrow	FISP	White-breasted Nuthatch	WBNU
Golden-winged Warbler	GWWA	White-eyed Vireo	WEVI
Grasshopper Sparrow	GRSP	Wild Turkey	WITU
Gray Catbird	GRCA	Wood Thrush	WOTH
Great Crested Flycatcher	GCFL	Worm-eating Warbler	WEWA
Great Horned Owl	GHOW	Yellow Warbler	YWAR
Greater Roadrunner	GRRO	Yellow-billed Cuckoo	YBCU
Hairy Woodpecker	HAWO	Yellow-breasted Chat	YBCH
Horned Lark	HOLA	Yellow-throated Vireo	YTVI
House Finch	HOFI	Yellow-throated Warbler	YTWA

Table C.9: Bird List for Pipestone National Monument, Minnesota.

Common Name	AOU Code	Common Name	AOU Code
Acadian Flycatcher	ACFL	Great Blue Heron	GBHE
American Bittern	AMBI	Great Crested Flycatcher	GCFL
American Coot	AMCO	Great Egret	GREG
American Crow	AMCR	Great Horned Owl	GHOW
American Goldfinch	AMGO	Green Heron	GRHE
American Kestrel	AMKE	Hairy Woodpecker	HAWO
American Redstart	AMRE	Henslow's Sparrow	HESP
American Robin	AMRO	Hooded Merganser	HOME
American Woodcock	AMWO	Horned Lark	HOLA
Bank Swallow	BANS	House Finch	HOFI
Barn Owl	BNOW	House Sparrow	HOSP
Barn Swallow	BARS	House Wren	HOWR
Barred Owl	BDOW	Indigo Bunting	INBU
Black-billed Cuckoo	BBCU	Killdeer	KILL
Black-capped Chickadee	BCCH	Lark Bunting	LABU
Black-crowned Night Heron	BCNH	Lark Sparrow	LASP
Black-tern	BLTE	Least Bittern	LEBI
Blue Grosbeak	BLGR	Least Flycatcher	LEFL
Blue Jay	BLJA	Little Blue Heron	LBHE
Blue-winged Teal	BWTE	Loggerhead Shrike	LOSH
Brewer's Blackbird	BRBL	Long-eared Owl	LEOW
Brown Thrasher	BRTH	Mallard	MALL
Brown-headed Cowbird	BHCO	Marsh Wren	MAWR
Canada Goose	CAGO	Mourning Dove	MODO
Cattle Egret	CAEG	Nashville Warbler	NAWA
Cedar Waxwing	CEDW	Northern Bobwhite	NOBO
Chimney Swift	CHSW	Northern Cardinal	NOCA
Chipping Sparrow	CHSP	Northern Flicker	NOFL
Clark's Grebe	CLGR	Northern Mockingbird	NOMO
Clay-colored Sparrow	CCSP	Northern Oriole	BAOR
Cliff Swallow	CLSW	Northern Pintail	NOPI
Common Grackle	COGR	Northern Rough-winged Swallow	NRWS
Common Morehead	COMO	Northern Shoveler	NSHO
Common Nighthawk	CONI	Orchard Oriole	OROR
Common Yellowthroat	COYE	Pied-billed Grebe	PBGR
Dickcissel	DICK	Pileated Woodpecker	PIWO
Double-crested Cormorant	DCCO	Purple Finch	PUFI
Downy Woodpecker	DOWO	Purple Martin	PUMA
Eared Grebe	EAGR	Red-bellied Woodpecker	RBWO
Eastern Bluebird	EABL	Red-eyed Vireo	REVI
Eastern Kingbird	EAKI	Red-headed Woodpecker	RHWO
Eastern Meadowlark	EAME	Red-shouldered Hawk	RSHA
Eastern Phoebe	EAPH	Red-tailed Hawk	RTHA
Eastern Screech Owl	EASO	Red-winged Blackbird	RWBL
Eastern Towhee	EATO	Ring-billed Gull	RBGU
Eastern Wood-Pewee	EAWP	Ring-necked Pheasant	RPHE
European Starling	EUST	Rock Dove	RODO
Field Sparrow	FISP	Ruby-throated Hummingbird	RTHU
Forster's Tern	FOTE	Ruddy Duck	RUDU
Gadwall	GADW	Savannah Sparrow	SAVS
Grasshopper Sparrow	GRSP	Sedge Wren	SEWR
Gray Catbird	GRCA	Short-eared Owl	SEOW
Gray Partridge	GRPA	Snowy Egret	SNEG
Gray-cheeked Thrush	GCTH	Song Sparrow	SOSP

Table C.9: Bird List for Pipestone National Monument, Minnesota - continued.

Common Name	AOU Code	Common Name	AOU Code
Sora	SORA	Wild Turkey	WITU
Swainson's Hawk	SWHA	Willow Flycatcher	WIFL
Swamp Sparrow	SWSP	Wilson's Phalarope	WIPH
Tree Swallow	TRES	Wood Duck	WODU
Turkey Vulture	TUVU	Yellow Warbler	YWAR
Upland Sandpiper	UPSA	Yellow-bellied Sapsucker	YBSA
Vesper Sparrow	VESP	Yellow-billed Cuckoo	YBCU
Warbling Vireo	WAVI	Yellow-breasted Chat	YBCH
Western Grebe	WEGR	Yellow-crowned Night Heron	YCNH
Western Kingbird	WEKI	Yellow-headed Blackbird	YHBL
Western Meadowlark	WEME		

Table C.10: Bird List for Tallgrass Prairie National Preserve, Kansas.

Common Name	AOU Code	Common Name	AOU Code
Acadian Flycatcher	ACFL	Great Horned Owl	GHOW
American Bittern	AMBI	Greater Prairie Chicken	GPCH
American Crow	AMCR	Great-tailed Grackle	GTGR
American Goldfinch	AMGO	Green Heron	GRHE
American Kestrel	AMKE	Hairy Woodpecker	HAWO
American Redstart	AMRE	Henslow's Sparrow	HESP
American Robin	AMRO	Horned Lark	HOLA
Bank Swallow	BANS	House Finch	HOFI
Barn Owl	BNOW	House Sparrow	HOSP
Barn Swallow	BARS	House Wren	HOWR
Barred Owl	BDOW	Indigo Bunting	INBU
Bell's Vireo	BEVI	Killdeer	KILL
Belted Kingbird	BEKI	Lark Sparrow	LASP
Bewick's Wren	BEWR	Little Blue Heron	LBHE
Black-and-White Warbler	BAWW	Loggerhead Shrike	LOSH
Black-billed Cuckoo	BBCU	Long-eared Owl	LEOW
Black-capped Chickadee	BCCH	Mallard	MALL
Black-crowned Night Heron	BCNH	Mourning Dove	MODO
Blue Grosbeak	BLGR	Northern Bobwhite	NOBO
Blue Jay	BLJA	Northern Cardinal	NOCA
Blue-gray Gnatcatcher	BGGN	Northern Flicker	NOFL
Blue-winged Teal	BWTE	Northern Harrier	NOHA
Bobolink	BOBO	Northern Mockingbird	NOMO
Brown Creeper	BRCR	Northern Oriole	BAOR
Brown Thrasher	BRTH	Northern Parula	NOPA
Brown-headed Cowbird	BHCO	Northern Rough-winged Swallow	NRWS
Burrowing Owl	BUOW	Orchard Oriole	OROR
Canada Goose	CAGO	Pied-billed Grebe	PBGR
Carolina Chickadee	CACH	Pileated Woodpecker	PIWO
Carolina Wren	CARW	Prairie Warbler	PRAW
Cattle Egret	CAEG	Prothonotary Warbler	PROW
Chimney Swift	CHSW	Purple Finch	PUFI
Chipping Sparrow	CHSP	Purple Martin	PUMA
Chuck-will's-widow	CWWI	Red-bellied Woodpecker	RBWO
Cliff Swallow	CLSW	Red-eyed Vireo	REVI
Common Grackle	COGR	Red-headed Woodpecker	RHWO
Common Nighthawk	CONI	Red-shouldered Hawk	RSHA
Common Yellowthroat	COYE	Red-tailed Hawk	RTHA
Dickcissel	DICK	Red-winged Blackbird	RWBL
Downy Woodpecker	DOWO	Ring-necked Pheasant	RPHE
Eastern Bluebird	EABL	Rock Dove	RODO
Eastern Kingbird	EAKI	Rose-breasted Grosbeak	RBGR
Eastern Meadowlark	EAME	Ruby-throated Hummingbird	RTHU
Eastern Phoebe	EAPH	Scarlet Tanager	SCTA
Eastern Screech Owl	EASO	Scissor-tailed Flycatcher	STFL
Eastern Towhee	EATO	Sedge Wren	SEWR
Eastern Wood-Pewee	EAWP	Semipalmated Sandpiper	SESA
European Starling	EUST	Summer Tanager	SUTA
Field Sparrow	FISP	Swainson's Hawk	SWHA
Grasshopper Sparrow	GRSP	Tuffed Titmouse	ETTI
Gray Catbird	GRCA	Turkey Vulture	TUVU
Great Blue Heron	GBHE	Upland Sandpiper	UPSA
Great Crested Flycatcher	GCFL	Veery	VEER
Great Egret	GREG	Vesper Sparrow	VESP

Table C.10: Bird List for Tallgrass Prairie National Preserve, Kansas - continued.

Common Name	AOU Code	Common Name	AOU Code
Warbling Vireo	WAVI	Wood Thrush	WOTH
Western Kingbird	WEKI	Yellow Warbler	YWAR
Western Meadowlark	WEME	Yellow-billed Cuckoo	YBCU
White-breasted Nuthatch	WBNU	Yellow-breasted Chat	YBCH
White-eyed Vireo	WEVI	Yellow-crowned Night Heron	YCNH
Wild Turkey	WITU	Yellow-throated Vireo	YTVI
Wood Duck	WODU		

Table C.11: Bird List for Wilson's Creek National Battlefield, Missouri.

Common Name	AOU Code	Common Name	AOU Code
Acadian Flycatcher	ACFL	Greater Roadrunner	GRRO
American Crow	AMCR	Green Heron	GRHE
American Goldfinch	AMGO	Hairy Woodpecker	HAWO
American Kestrel	AMKE	Hooded Merganser	HOME
American Redstart	AMRE	Hooded Warbler	HOWA
American Robin	AMRO	Horned Lark	HOLA
American Woodcock	AMWO	House Finch	HOFI
Bank Swallow	BANS	House Sparrow	HOSP
Barn Owl	BNOW	House Wren	HOWR
Barn Swallow	BARS	Indigo Bunting	INBU
Barred Owl	BDOW	Kentucky Warbler	KEWA
Bell's Vireo	BEVI	Killdeer	KILL
Belted Kingbird	BEKI	Lark Sparrow	LASP
Bewick's Wren	BEWR	Least Bittern	LEBI
Black-and-White Warbler	BAWW	Loggerhead Shrike	LOSH
Black-billed Cuckoo	BBCU	Long-eared Owl	LEOW
Black-crowned Night Heron	BCNH	Louisiana Waterthrush	LOWA
Blue Grosbeak	BLGR	Mallard	MALL
Blue Jay	BLJA	Mourning Dove	MODO
Blue-gray Gnatcatcher	BGGN	Northern Bobwhite	NOBO
Blue-winged Teal	BWTE	Northern Cardinal	NOCA
Blue-winged Warbler	BWWA	Northern Flicker	YSFL
Broad-winged Hawk	BWHA	Northern Harrier	NOHA
Brown Thrasher	BRTH	Northern Mockingbird	NOMO
Brown-headed Cowbird	BHCO	Northern Oriole	BAOR
Canada Goose	CAGO	Northern Parula	NOPA
Carolina Chickadee	CACH	Northern Rough-winged Swallow	NRWS
Carolina Wren	CARW	Orchard Oriole	OROR
Cattle Egret	CAEG	Ovenbird	OVEN
Cerulean Warbler	CERW	Painted Bunting	PABU
Chimney Swift	CHSW	Pileated Woodpecker	PIWO
Chipping Sparrow	CHSP	Pine Warbler	PIWA
Chuck-will's-widow	CWWI	Prairie Warbler	PRAW
Cliff Swallow	CLSW	Prothonotary Warbler	PROW
Common Grackle	COGR	Purple Finch	PUFI
Common Nighthawk	CONI	Purple Martin	PUMA
Common Yellowthroat	COYE	Red-bellied Woodpecker	RBWO
Dickcissel	DICK	Red-eyed Vireo	REVI
Downy Woodpecker	DOWO	Red-headed Woodpecker	RHWO
Eastern Bluebird	EABL	Red-shouldered Hawk	RSHA
Eastern Kingbird	EAKI	Red-tailed Hawk	RTHA
Eastern Meadowlark	EAME	Red-winged Blackbird	RWBL
Eastern Phoebe	EAPH	Rock Dove	RODO
Eastern Screech Owl	EASO	Rose-breasted Grosbeak	RBGR
Eastern Towhee	EATO	Ruby-throated Hummingbird	RTHU
Eastern Wood-Pewee	EAWP	Scarlet Tanager	SCTA
European Starling	EUST	Scissor-tailed Flycatcher	STFL
Field Sparrow	FISP	Snowy Egret	SNEG
Golden-winged Warbler	GWWA	Song Sparrow	SOSP
Grasshopper Sparrow	GRSP	Summer Tanager	SUTA
Gray Catbird	GRCA	Tree Swallow	TRES
Great Blue Heron	GBHE	Tuffed Titmouse	ETTI
Great Crested Flycatcher	GCFL	Turkey Vulture	TUVU
Great Horned Owl	GHOW	Warbling Vireo	WAVI

Table C.11: Bird List for Wilson's Creek National Battlefield, Missouri – continued.

Common Name	AOU Code	Common Name	AOU Code
Whip-poor-will	WPWI	Worm-eating Warbler	WEWA
White-breasted Nuthatch	WBNU	Yellow Warbler	YWAR
White-eyed Vireo	WEVI	Yellow-billed Cuckoo	YBCU
Wild Turkey	WITU	Yellow-breasted Chat	YBCH
Willow Flycatcher	WIFL	Yellow-crowned Night Heron	YCNH
Wood Duck	WODU	Yellow-throated Vireo	YTVI
Wood Thrush	WOTH	Yellow-throated Warbler	YTWA

Appendix D. Evaluation of Habitat Data as Correlates of Bird Community Metrics and Species Occurrence

Lloyd W. Morrison

Quantitative Ecologist,

Heartland Inventory and Monitoring Network

National Park Service

Final version

9 April 2007

BACKGROUND

The purpose of these analyses is to evaluate the value of habitat data collected in conjunction with bird community monitoring at several HTLN parks. Different habitat types are recognized at each park, and it was desired to have the data analyzed separately for each park/habitat type (hereafter "PHT). Annual sample sizes for most PHTs are relatively small. Only at the TAPR and AGFO upland habitats were annual sample sizes > 20. Because a rotating panel is employed at the TAPR upland PHT, the total sample size is larger for this PHT. Data were not pooled across years for analyses involving this PHT, however, as inter-annual variability would likely bias the results. A total of 32 habitat variables were included for evaluation. Data were collected for all variables in each PHT (in most years), even if the habitat of interest was not present (i.e., only 0's were recorded).

PHT	Annual Sample Size
AGFO-riparian	14
AGFO-upland	13-40
HEHO-upland	9
HOCU-riparian	5
HOCU-upland	20
HOCU-edge	2
TAPR-riparian	16-18
TAPR-upland	79-242

EVALUATION OF INDIVIDUAL HABITAT VARIABLES

I evaluated all habitat variables made available to me (n=32) for AGFO and TAPR. Separate evaluations were made for riparian corridor and upland habitats. Five years of data were available for both parks and habitat types. In-depth analyses were conducted for the first and last years (2001 and 2006) for each data set. If results differed dramatically between the two years, the intervening years were examined.

Analyses consisted of examining the data range and distribution of each habitat variable for each park, habitat type, and year separately. Habitat variables were then classified according to their likely information content in correlational analyses with bird species data.

Definitions of groupings:

Uninformative: Data consisted of all or mostly 0's for the variable of interest. In other words, that particular habitat type wasn't present at any or at most sites.

Questionable: Distribution of data highly skewed, many small or large values, or an otherwise narrow data range; transformations necessary for any analyses requiring a normal distribution of data. May only be informative as predictors of occurrence (e.g., logistic regression) rather than abundance. **Or** this variable may meet the definition of potentially informative in some years and be considered uninformative in others, not a consistently useful variable.

Potentially Informative: Good data range and distribution near normal or likely to be transformed to normal or near normal.

It should be noted that a number of variables appeared to be reasonably informative in some years and not in others. This may be partially due in part to natural inter-annual variability, and in part to the fact that many of the sites sampled each year were different. Whatever the reason, this aspect of the data set needs to be emphasized. Although I have made an effort to summarize the usefulness of each variable generally, prior to conducting in-depth analyses with specific habitat variables it would be wise to examine each year of data.

Note: HVPB = Horizontal Vegetation Profile Board

AGFO--Riparian Corridor

Uninformative
Canopy height
Canopy cover
Basal area
Conifer litter
Rock
Woody debris
Moss & lichen
Shrubs & vines
Tree seedlings
Warm season grass
HVPB 5-m;1.25m
HVPB 5-m;1.50m
HVPB 5-m;1.75m
HVPB 5-m;2.00m
HVPB 15-m;1.25m
HVPB 15-m;1.50m
HVPB 15-m;1.75m
HVPB 15-m;2.00m

Questionable
Deciduous litter
HVPB 5-m;1.00m
HVPB 15-m;1.00m

Potentially Informative
Grass litter
Bare soil

Unvegetated
Cool season grass
Forbs
Total foliar cover
HVPB 5-m;0.50m
HVPB 5-m;0.75m
HVPB 15-m;0.50m
HVPB 15-m;0.75m
H

AGFO--Upland

Uninformative
Canopy height
Canopy cover
Basal area
Deciduous litter
Conifer litter
Woody debris
Tree seedlings
HVPB 5-m;1.00m
HVPB 5-m;1.25m
HVPB 5-m;1.50m
HVPB 5-m;1.75m
HVPB 5-m;2.00m
HVPB 15-m;1.00m
HVPB 15-m;1.25m
HVPB 15-m;1.50m
HVPB 15-m;1.75m
HVPB 15-m;2.00m

Questionable
Rock
Unvegetated
Moss & lichen
Shrubs & vines
Warm season grass
HVPB 5-m;0.75m
HVPB 15-m;0.75m
H

Potentially Informative
Grass litter
Bare soil
Cool season grass
Forbs

Total foliar cover
HVPB 5-m;0.50m
HVPB 15-m;0.50m

TAPR--Riparian Corridor

Uninformative
Conifer litter

Questionable
Rock
Woody debris
Moss & lichen
Shrubs & vines
Tree seedlings
Warm season grass
HVPB 5-m;0.50m
HVPB 5-m;0.75m
HVPB 5-m;1.25m
HVPB 5-m;1.50m
HVPB 5-m;1.75m
HVPB 5-m;2.00m
HVPB 15-m;0.50m
HVPB 15-m;0.75m
HVPB 15-m;1.25m
HVPB 15-m;1.50m
HVPB 15-m;1.75m
HVPB 15-m;2.00m

Potentially Informative
Canopy height
Canopy cover
Basal area
Deciduous litter
Grass litter
Bare soil
Unvegetated
Cool season grass
Forbs
Total foliar cover
HVPB 5-m;1.00m
HVPB 15-m;1.00m
H

TAPR--Upland

Uninformative
Canopy height
Canopy cover
Basal area
Conifer litter
Woody debris
Tree seedlings
HVPB 5-m;1.25m
HVPB 5-m;1.50m
HVPB 5-m;1.75m
HVPB 5-m;2.00m
HVPB 15-m;1.25m
HVPB 15-m;1.50m
HVPB 15-m;1.75m
HVPB 15-m;2.00m

Questionable
Deciduous litter
Grass litter
Rock
Unvegetated
Cool season grass
Moss & lichen
Shrubs & vines
HVPB 5-m;0.75m
HVPB 5-m;1.00m
HVPB 15-m;0.75m
HVPB 15-m;1.00m
H

Potentially Informative
Bare soil
Forbs
Total foliar cover
Warm season grass
HVPB 5-m;0.50m
HVPB 15-m;0.50m

ANALYSES

The large number of predictor variables and small sample size extremely limits the statistical approaches that can be employed (at least that could include most or all habitat variables). Stepwise multiple linear or logistic regression analyses are frequently used as model-building approaches when the goal is to select a small set of informative predictors from a large number of potentially intercorrelated variables. Factor analyses are often employed prior to such analyses to reduce a large number of predictor variables to a smaller set of derived, uncorrelated variables. A combination of factor analysis followed by stepwise multiple linear regression, and stepwise multiple logistic regression was applied to the bird data to evaluate habitat correlates. Minimum sample sizes necessary for these types of analyses precluded their application to most PHTs.

Method Minimum	sample size	Reference
Multiple linear regression analyses	10-20 for each predictor variable	Harrell 2002
Multiple logistic regression analyses	At least 10 EPV, where EPV = the smaller of the counts for the values of the binary variable/the number of predictor variables	Peduzzi et al. 1996
Factor analysis	Depends on various things; 10 per variable to 300 overall	MacCallum et al. 1999

In interpretation of the following analyses, it should be kept in mind that all such sequential (i.e., stepwise) methods suffer from compromised Type I error rates, as many variables are considered for inclusion simultaneously. Also, it must be remembered that correlation is not causation. It has been demonstrated using synthetic data that "significant" models may be constructed from data sets in which there are no functional relationships between the response and predictor variables (Mac Nally 2000).

Determinants of bird community metrics

Multivariate approach

The first approach was to focus on a metric of overall bird communities, and species richness was used as the response variable. It was desirable to evaluate as many predictor variables in the models as possible. A multiple linear regression analysis could not be employed on the raw data because of sample size limitations. A factor analysis was run for the TAPR upland PHT in 2006. The sample size was too small for this analysis according to information published in the literature (although within the range of analyses in other published studies).

The statistical algorithm used to extract factors was a principal components analysis. This method forms linear combinations from the observed variables, resulting in a smaller number of derived variables. The first principle component is the combination that accounts for the largest amount of variance in the sample. Only the components with eigenvalues greater than one were retained. This resulted in five principal components that explained a cumulative variance of 77.5%. An orthogonal rotation was performed to increase ease of interpretation.

The five principal components were then used as predictor variables in a multiple linear regression analysis with bird species number as the response variable. The sample size was entirely within the specified limits for this type of analysis. A forward stepwise selection process was used, with a default criteria of $p = 0.05$ for variable inclusion and $p = 0.10$ for variable removal. None of the principal components was selected as a significant predictor.

Univariate approach

The next step was to evaluate all pairwise correlations of habitat and bird community variables. A Spearman correlation coefficient was used as most habitat variables did not appear to come from a normal distribution. This was done for the AGFO upland and riparian and TAPR upland and riparian PHTs in 2006. Surprisingly, this analysis revealed very few "significant" correlations among species richness and any of the habitat variables:

Significant habitat correlates of bird species richness:

TAPR upland 2006: (n=1) moss and lichen, r = 0.227
TAPR riparian 2006: (n=1) cool season grass, r = 0.487
AGFO upland 2006: (n=1) forbs, r = -0.485
AGFO riparian 2006: (n=8) total foliar cover, r=0.538; 7 HVPB variables, all negative correlations, highest r = -0.649

Similar results were obtained with diversity as the response variable (diversity and species richness were highly positively correlated; r always > 0.95).

Because so many multiple comparisons were made simultaneously, the probability of a type I error is no longer 0.05. Some sort of correction for multiple comparisons should be made or, alternatively, this analysis could be viewed as "descriptive" rather than inferential, and potentially biologically important variables identified based on the size of the correlation coefficients. Comparisons of p-values among PHTs should not be done, as the PHTs have different sample sizes, and p-values are dependent upon sample size.

Conclusions from these analyses:

(1) The sample sizes will be too small for multiple linear regression analyses or factor analyses (except possibly for upland sites at TAPR when only a small number of predictor variables are included).

(2) Very few "significant" correlations of bird community metrics with habitat variables were observed by pairwise comparisons, and few of them were very strong. Correcting for multiple comparisons will likely result in no "significant" habitat correlates for most PHTs.

(3) Simple pairwise comparisons may be the best way of evaluating habitat correlates in terms of community level metrics, at least in a descriptive manner.

Determinants of species occurrence

I evaluated species occurrence patterns at AGFO and TAPR with a stepwise multiple logistic regression. A forward stepwise selection process was employed, using the score statistic for evaluating variables for entry into the model, and the conditional statistic for evaluating variables for removal.

A list of birds from each PHT was specified as follows (D. Peitz, email correspondence):

AGFO: GRSP, LASP, MODO, RWBL, and WEME.

TAPR: BARS, BHCO, BRTH, CONI, DICK, EAKI, GRSP, KILL, LASP, RWBL, UPSA, and WEME.

A list of species was also provided for other PHTs, although small sample sizes precluded multiple logistic regression analyses.

It was indicated that the "potentially informative" habitat variables determined earlier should be included in these analyses, as well as the "questionable" variables, to see how the resulting models might be influenced (D. Peitz, email correspondence). Thus two sets of models were constructed for each PHT, one including only the "potentially informative" habitat variables, and one including the "potentially informative" habitat variables and the "questionable" variables. Analyses were run for upland sites at TAPR and AGFO in 2006. The habitat variables [HVPB 5-m;0.50m] and [HVPB 15-m;0.50m] were among the "potentially informative" variables for both PHTs, and the remaining HVPB variables designated as "questionable" were not included in the analyses, as the HVPB variables were in general highly intercorrelated.

It is difficult to obtain an informative model for species present at only a few sites or species present at almost all sites. Thus the following species were removed from consideration because they were too rare: BARS, BRTH, EAKI, and LASP at TAPR; or too common: WEME at TAPR and AGFO.

Total sample sizes were clearly too small for such a large number of predictor variables, and the resulting models are not expected to be stable. The output, however, allows a univariate examination of each of the independent variables, which is informative and recommended as the first step in any logistic model building process (Hosmer and Lemeshow 2000). The coefficients for each predictor variable considered alone will not vary with the total number of predictor variables considered.

Summary measures for evaluating the goodness of fit for a logistic multiple regression include the Cox Snell R^2 and Nagelkerke R^2. The interpretation of these measures is not the same as the coefficient of determination in a linear regression however, and in general they are difficult to interpret (Norusis 2000). The percent of correct classification is another summary measure that is often used, but it is actually a poor indicator of model fit. It is possible to add highly significant variables to the model, yet have the correct classification rate decline, as was observed in some cases with this data set.

Results:

The interpretation of the logistic regression models is that the probability of a bird species being present at a site is $1/(1+e^{-Z})$, where Z is equal to the equations given for each species.

At AGFO, including only "potentially informative" habitat variables (n=7), the results were:

RWBL: -1.960 + 0.145 forbs

No significant predictors were found for LASP, MODO, or GRSP.

At AGFO, including both "potentially informative" and "questionable" habitat variables (n=12; additional HPVB variables were not included since HVPB 5-m; 0.50m and HVPB 15-m; 0.50m were included and were highly correlated with the other HPVB variables), the results were:

GRSP: -0.662 + 0.183 warm season grass
RWBL: 11.147 + 0.183 forbs – 9.957 H

No significant predictors were found for LASP or MODO.

At TAPR in 2006, including only "potentially informative" habitat variables (n=6), the results were:

DICK: -2.821 + 0.047 HVPB 15-m; 0.50m
GRSP: -0.235 + 0.043 warm season grass
KILL: 0.865 – 0.051 HVPB 5-m; 0.50m

No significant predictors were found for BARS, BHCO, CONI, RWBL, or UPSA.

At TAPR, including both "potentially informative" and "questionable" habitat variables (n=14; additional HPVB variables were not included since HVPB 5-m; 0.50m and HVPB 15-m; 0.50m were included and were highly correlated with the other HPVB variables), the results were:

DICK: -12.374 + 0.053 HVPB 15-m; 0.50m + 0.108 unvegetated + 0.096 grass litter - 0.117 forbs
GRSP: -0.363 – 0.129 cool season grass + 0.037 total foliar cover
KILL: 0.865 – 0.051 HVPB 5-m;0.50m
RWBL: -1.182 + 0.046 cool season grass
UPSA: 0.637 - 0.062 cool season grass

No significant predictors were found for BARS, BHCO, or CONI.

Note that for both AGFO and TAPR, the selection of predictor variables in the models was dependent upon the set of variables entered into the model building process.

This analysis was also conducted for TAPR upland sites in 2001, as an assessment of model validation. Including only "potentially informative" habitat variables (n=6), the results were:

DICK: -11.385 + 0.098 HVPB 15-m; 0.50m + 0.035 Bare Soil + 0.017 HVPB 5-m;0.50m
GRSP: 0.072 + 0.032 warm season grass
RWBL: -4.248 – 0.133 warm season grass + 0.066 total foliar cover
UPSA: -3.00 + 0.038 bare soil

No significant predictors were found for BARS, BHCO, CONI, or KILL.

Comparing these results to the same PHT in 2006, with only the "potentially informative" habitat variables (n=6) used in both analyses, it is obvious that different models were the result. Some species had significant models in one year but not in the other. This indicates these models in general are not stable, have very low predictive value, and are not applicable to areas of the park that were not included in the respective sample.

Conclusions from these analyses:

(1) The sample sizes will be too small for multiple logistic regression analyses (except possibly for upland sites at TAPR when only a small number of predictor variables are included).

(2) The models presented here are not the only, nor necessarily the "best" models for a given species. Many different options for model building are available, and the options selected, along with the habitat variables included, can potentially produce many different models. Any given model building algorithm cannot guarantee a "best" model in a statistical sense, and the choice of a model will ultimately depend upon factors such as objectives of the study, ease of variable acquisition, and interpretation (Norusis 2003).

(3) The resulting models are likely to vary among years (i.e., panel of sample sites), indicating low predictive value. This is a result of a small sample size and may also result from interannual variability, heterogeneity across different sampling sites, or problems with the sampling design.

(4) The most informative use of multiple logistic regression analyses is likely to be a focused study on one or a few species, rather than trying to construct models for a relatively large number of species in each PHT. The most informative model building will result from careful evaluation of all habit variables based on the natural history of the species and the issues associated with each PHT. If certain habitat variables are known to be important for the species of interest, they should be included in the model regardless of their significance level (Norusis 2003). Competing models should be evaluated (both statistically and practically) and the most informative model or models determined. This process should include evaluation of model diagnostics (not done here) and model validation.

SUMMARY CONCLUSIONS AND RECOMMENDATIONS

There are other, more sophisticated methods that could be applied to this data, although the large number of potential predictor variables coupled with the relatively small sample sizes will be a problem with any multivariate analyses. With any model building approach, the results of the model will be dependent upon the subset of predictor variables chosen for evaluation.

Overall conclusions

Assuming the five-minute surveys accurately depict the bird species composition of a given site, the general lack of basic explanatory power for the habitat variables may be due to two potential sources:

(1) Because parks have already been divided into different habitat types, there may be too much homogeneity within each habitat type. The data for a number of habitat variables exhibit a narrow range of values, supporting this hypothesis.

(2) The territory or home range of the bird species may be larger than the area sampled for habitat, or have a low degree of overlap with the area sampled for habitat (i.e., habitat data are sampled out to 50m from the plot center, but birds are observed out to 100 m). If the scale of the birds' territory or home range is not similar to the scale over which habitat is measured, or if the two do not overlap to a large degree, the habitat data may not be representative of the bird species in question. This is likely to be a larger problem for some species than others.

Recommendations

I have the following overall recommendations:

(1) Reduce the collection of habitat data and reallocate the time to collecting more bird data, by sampling more sites when possible. The habitat data, as currently collected, do not appear to be very useful as correlates of overall bird community metrics or consistent predictors of species occurrence. Collecting habitat data from multiple subplots at a site probably does not yield more accurate information than collecting habitat data from a single plot.

(2) Instead of collecting a wide variety of generalized habitat data, focus on a suite of habitat variables likely to be important to each of a small group of target bird species. This will require knowledge of the natural history of the species involved, as well as the management issues and goals of each park or PHT with reference to the bird species. Such an approach seems necessary for informative model building.

(3) The most informative use of the data as currently collected may be the estimation of habitat parameters on a PHT scale, and evaluation of change in these parameters over time. It may be possible to correlate overall long-term changes in the abundance of target bird species (within a PHT) with changes in certain habitat variables.

REFERENCES

Harrell, F.E. (2001) *Regression modeling strategies: With applications to linear models, logistic regression, and survival analysis.* New York and Berlin, Springer.

Hosmer, D.W. and Lemeshow, S. (2000) *Applied logistic regression*. New York, John Wiley and Sons.

Mac Nally, R. (2000) Regression and model-building in conservation biology, biogeography and ecology: The distinction between--and reconciliation of--'predictive' and 'explanatory' models. *Biodiversity and Conservation* **9**: 655-671.

MacCallum, R.C., Widaman, K.F., Zhang, S. and Hong, S. (1999) Sample size in factor analysis. *Psychological Methods* **4**: 84-99.

Norusis, M.J. (2003) *SPSS 12.0 Statistical Procedures Companion*. Upper Saddle River, New Jersey, Prentice Hall.

Peduzzi, P.N., Concato, J., Kemper, E., Holford, T.R. and Feinstein, A. (1996) A simulation study of the number of events per variable in logistic regression analysis. *Journal of Clinical Epidemiology* **99**: 1373-1379.

The NPS has organized its parks with significant natural resources into 32 networks linked by geography and shared natural resource characteristics. HTLN is composed of 15 National Park Service (NPS) units in eight Midwestern states. These parks contain a wide variety of natural and cultural resources including sites focused on commemorating civil war battlefields, Native American heritage, westward expansion, and our U.S. Presidents. The Network is charged with creating inventories of its species and natural features as well as monitoring trends and issues in order to make sound management decisions. Critical inventories help park managers understand the natural resources in their care while monitoring programs help them understand meaningful change in natural systems and to respond accordingly. The Heartland Network helps to link natural and cultural resources by protecting the habitat of our history.

The I&M program bridges the gap between science and management with a third of its efforts aimed at making information accessible. Each network of parks, such as Heartland, has its own multi-disciplinary team of scientists, support personnel, and seasonal field technicians whose system of online databases and reports make information and research results available to all. Greater efficiency is achieved through shared staff and funding as these core groups of professionals augment work done by individual park staff. Through this type of integration and partnership, network parks are able to accomplish more than a single park could on its own.

The mission of the Heartland Network is to collaboratively develop and conduct scientifically credible inventories and long-term monitoring of park "vital signs" and to distribute this information for use by park staff, partners, and the public, thus enhancing understanding which leads to sound decision making in the preservation of natural resources and cultural history held in trust by the National Park Service.

www.nature.nps.gov/im/units/htln/

The Department of the Interior protects and manages the nation's natural resources and cultural heritage; provides scientific and other information about those resources; and honors its special responsibilities to American Indians, Alaska Natives, and affiliated Island Communities.

NPS D-78, May 2008